TURNER **CLASSIC** MOVIES.

Must-See Musicals

50 SHOW-STOPPING MOVIES
WE CAN'T FORGET

RICHARD BARRIOS

FOREWORD BY MICHAEL FEINSTEIN

RUNNING PRESS

PHILADELPHIA

For Tootsie
"And you know I love you, too!"

Running Press
Hachette Book Group
1290 Avenue of the Americas, New York, NY 10104
www.runningpress.com
@Running_Press

Printed in China
First Edition: October 2017

Published by Running Press, an imprint of Perseus Books, LLC, a subsidiary of Hachette Book Group, Inc.

The Hachette Speakers Bureau provides a wide range of authors for speaking events.
To find out more, go to www.hachettespeakersbureau.com or call (866) 376-6591.

The publisher is not responsible for websites (or their content) that are not owned by the publisher.

Print book cover and interior design by Joshua McDonnell.

Library of Congress Control Number: 2017942847
ISBNs: 978-0-7624-6316-9 (paperback), 978-0-7624-6317-6 (ebook)
1010
10 9 8 7 6 5 4 3 2 1

Fred Astaire and Ginger Rogers, "Cheek to Cheek," *Top Hat* (1935)

CONTENTS

Foreword
by Michael Feinstein

It takes many things to make a movie musical. Money, of course, but also much that cannot carry a price tag: imagination, ingenuity, audacity, wisdom, experience, creativity, energy, courage. Most of all, it takes talent, which can manifest itself in all sorts of ways. There are the inherent and intuitive gifts of a great artist, the learned skills of a master technician, and everything in between. Without an abundance of talent in every department and category, a musical film will never fly, let alone become one that can carry the label "Must-See." Yet, despite these staggering requirements and achievements, it must be noted that during the so-called Golden Age of the Movie Musical—roughly the mid-1930s to the mid-1950s—talent was often, if not usually, taken for granted. With a studio such as MGM, in its busiest years turning out one feature film per week, those in charge could rule over even the most exceptionally gifted employees with a "factory" mindset. Those who worked both before and behind the camera were contracted, salaried, and often unappreciated, producing work which far too often was accepted but not necessarily prized. Andre Previn, who began working at MGM while still in his teens, commented on this situation very pointedly. From the perspective of the studio bosses, he said, "the music department was no more or less important than the department of fake lawns."

Fortunately, the artists themselves did not feel that way toward their work. They took pride in what they did, and the films they made gloriously demonstrate that this pride was very much justified. It's only in retrospect, in fact, that we can now fully appreciate the magnitude of talent that went into creating the greatest musicals. It should be stressed, too, that this talent was not borne only by the biggest names in the movie credits, by the Astaires and Garlands and Kellys and Days. Other people working in musicals may have had far less name recognition, but possessed equal gifts. My particular heroes in musicals have names that are unknown to most viewers, since the results of their specific genius were heard, not seen. Composers, orchestrators, conductors, and arrangers such as Roger Edens, Conrad Salinger, Herbert Spencer, Skip Martin, Kay Thompson, David Raksin, Saul Chaplin, Lennie Hayton, and Edward Powell are, for me, the invisible giants who have informed the sensibility I have in approaching music. I will always be grateful to them, and for them.

Just about all of the best musical films have something in common: their greatness is more apparent now than was the case when they were new. As perspective makes clear, these movies are far from frivolous, and vastly more substantial than originally thought. Even now, they don't always get the respect they deserve, yet nonetheless have an effect which can be profound. By using a sort of fantasy kaleidoscope, they reflect society's dreams, ideals, and yearnings, capturing an honesty that is tremendously genuine. A film such as *The Band Wagon* uses a vast amount of artistry and spectacle, in both sight and sound, to say things which are, at the heart of the matter, personal and meaningful. The extraordinary quality of the work on display might make it easy to momentarily forget that we're being told fundamental human truths, but they come through regardless.

Especially in these times of devalued appreciation for art in general, musicals will continue to be significant, to inspire wonder and devotion in each succeeding generation. Best of all, these generations will then be moved to create fresh and outstanding work. So it is that "Must-See Musicals," old and new, will keep on going. They are, in a magnificent kind of way, eternal.

Introduction

A man so elated that he sings and dances through a downpour. A girl with a dog, wondering about life beyond her Kansas farm. A painted master of ceremonies in a sinister cabaret. A young woman who isn't cut out to be a nun. A pair of murderesses who wow the crowds as they strut while waving machine guns. A couple in Los Angeles who might fall in love while they dance. Chorus line formations, dancing gang members, and Americans in Paris.

These are all memorable images, and the sounds that accompany them are equally unforgettable. They are, of course, just a few moments from a fabulous and fascinating—if sometimes peculiar—body of work we call movie musicals. For the millions who care about them, musicals are like comfort food without the calories and intoxication without the hangover. They can turn depression into joy and burdens into blessings, and the pleasure they offer usually contains no guilt. They imply that dreams can come true or are at least reasonable, and hold the possibility that perhaps we too can express our feelings by dancing like Astaire or singing like Streisand.

Musicals are special, too, in that not everyone appreciates them, nor understands those who do. In fact, one reason they have gone in and out of fashion so often is because it takes a particular, and not always prevalent, mind-set to comprehend and embrace them. But don't ever count them out; every single time people think they're over, a new song-and-dance phoenix will rise to show just how resilient they can be, and

how wonderful.

From the late 1920s to now and beyond, musical films have been extraordinarily adept at communicating with their audiences and connecting them with both current tastes and timeless aspirations. In their nine decades of existence, they have been indelible and necessary, and scores of them are classics—although perhaps that word *scores* needs examination. It may be that the musical "best of the best," the collection of titles that are truly great, is not as large a group as one might imagine. Lots of them have one or two wonderful numbers or scenes but also a great deal of uninspired filler. There are many where the script is not nearly as compelling as the music, and some where good intentions were followed by dismaying results. It takes enormous effort to produce a musical that is genuinely good in its entirety, and, of course, there's that built-in proviso under which every musical must operate: the harder it works, the easier it must make it all seem. They take an enormous amount of preparation and engineering, and for the most part must disguise all of it in a brightly colored haze of effortlessness. For one to sustain its quality all the way through to the end, in the manner of, say, a *Singin' in the Rain*, is far more difficult than might be imagined.

How many musicals truly have the elusive mix of qualities that it takes to be considered a classic? In this book, fifty have been singled out. A roster of this sort, subjective as it is, must necessarily take some major factors into consideration. Some titles, like *Meet Me in St. Louis* or

Top Hat, are an easy call, loved by nearly everyone. There are also those that have been so wildly successful and widely seen that for some people they symbolize *all* movie musicals; *The Sound of Music* and *Grease* are good examples. Others are historically significant, artistically enterprising, or profoundly influential, and there are a few that may be less familiar to many. There are no hard and fast guidelines governing these choices, and in one or two cases it was nearly heartbreaking to remove a contender. Every entry was considered and debated and weighed in the balance, and ultimately the judgments are based on a number of factors, tastes, and quirks. Just like the films themselves.

A few words need be said about some inclusions or omissions that can be considered arguable. Where, for instance, is Al Jolson in *The Jazz Singer* (1927)? Apart from the fact that it's not a very good movie, it's less a musical than it is a mostly silent film with some songs. Speaking of popular stars, people like Alice Faye, Eleanor Powell, Nelson Eddy, and Betty Grable worked mainly in films that were essentially products of their time, entertaining then and now without being terribly exceptional or resonant. *The Red Shoes* (1948) and *Lili* (1953) are brilliant but not really musicals, and a film like *Easter Parade* (1948) is delightful without being very innovative—much of what it achieves overlaps works that are ultimately more significant. As for more recent hits like *Mamma Mia!* (2008)

Seven Brides for Seven Brothers "Goin' Co'tin'": Marc Platt, Jane Powell, Jeff Richards, Russ Tamblyn, Jacques D'Amboise, Tommy Rall, Matt Mattox

or *Les Misérables* (2012), they can be considered a matter of taste, essentially, as many musicals can be. The same with older films such as *South Pacific* (1958) and *Camelot* (1967) which, just like politics, elicit strong reactions on both sides of the aisle. And why not more foreign films? Well, some of them may be "interesting" as opposed to truly successful, and many that are more enterprising can be judged a genre apart from this mainstream, thus deserving of their own in-depth study. There may be a work or performer whose inclusion might raise an eyebrow or two: just remember, then, that what some

musicals may lack in artistry, they make up for in influence, success, and relevance.

It must always be recalled that musicals, with their many repercussions, are about their audiences as much as their performers. That certainty guarantees that most readers will not likely be in complete agreement with this present list, nor mollified by the "More to See" supplementary titles in every listing. For those who feel compelled to make her or his own list of top titles: hallelujah, get busy, and go for it. Just remember, while doing so, that musicals are a big-tent kind of genre; as long as everyone

The Sound of Music "Edelweiss": Christopher Plummer, Charmian Carr, Kym Karath, Julie Andrews, Angela Cartwright, Nicholas Hammond, Heather Menzies, Duane Chase, Eleanor Parker

keeps a civil disposition and a sense of humor, we can rejoice when we concur and agree to disagree when we don't. Even about *Moulin Rouge!* (2001) or *The Pirate* (1948) or any other that might draw an especially passionate response, pro or con. After all, when a musical has done its job, an impassioned viewer may be quite a fitting result.

Given that musical films are aural as well as visual, there may be only so much that a book can do to evoke and commemorate them. Still, it is hoped that between the text and the illustrations, *Turner Classic Movies: Must-See Musicals* can be seen as an appropriate salute to these glorious and engaging works. Each one has its own particular quality, its special backstory, its unique path to the summit. Most or all of them should be watched and rewatched, discussed and debated and, in many instances, truly loved. Musicals are made, first and foremost, to be enjoyed by their audiences. Those that succeed in this goal are touched by a very particular kind of magic. Thus, it is with gratitude and affection—and occasionally with a question or comment—that this book applauds the artists who created these musicals. Even more than that, it celebrates the pleasure and delight they will forever continue to bestow.

THE BROADWAY MELODY

MGM, 1929 | **BLACK AND WHITE/COLOR (TECHNICOLOR), 100 MINUTES**

DIRECTOR: **HARRY BEAUMONT**   PRODUCERS: **HARRY RAPF, IRVING THALBERG, LAWRENCE WEINGARTEN (UNCREDITED)**
SCREENPLAY: **EDMUND GOULDING (STORY), SARAH Y. MASON (CONTINUITY), NORMAN HOUSTON AND JAMES GLEASON (DIALOGUE)**
SONGS: **NACIO HERB BROWN (MUSIC) AND ARTHUR FREED (LYRICS)**   CHOREOGRAPHER: **GEORGE CUNNINGHAM (UNCREDITED)**
STARRING: **CHARLES KING (EDDIE KEARNS), ANITA PAGE (QUEENIE MAHONEY), BESSIE LOVE (HANK MAHONEY), JED PROUTY
(UNCLE JED), KENNETH THOMSON (WARRINER), MARY DORAN (FLO), EDDIE KANE (FRANCIS ZANFIELD), DREW DEMOREST (TURPE,
COSTUME DESIGNER), JOYCE MURRAY (SPECIALTY DANCER), JAMES GLEASON (MUSIC PUBLISHER)**

Both members of a small-time sister act find love and disappointment after making it into a Broadway show.

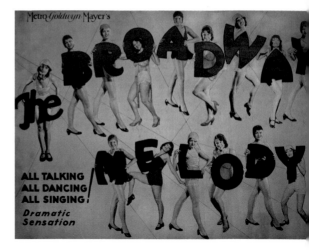

To quote a later musical (specifically, *The Sound of Music*), let's start at the very beginning. Where song-and-dance films are concerned, Square One is occupied by *The Broadway Melody*. The screen's first real musical, it is responsible for everything that would follow. Everything.

Al Jolson's *The Jazz Singer* and *The Singing Fool* were crucial in bringing sound to movies; *The Broadway Melody* showed the world that they could sing and dance. At a time when other studios and filmmakers were struggling to solve the mysteries of sound, MGM boldly harnessed the new medium to create its first "all-talking" film, an out-and-out original musical. Based

loosely on the real-life Duncan Sisters, it was greeted as the finest sound film yet made, seen and loved by millions. Its impact was immediate, and its influence and repercussions were so vast that by April 1930, when it won the Academy Award for Best Picture (or, as the Academy then called it, Outstanding Picture), it was both legendary and on its way to being obsolete.

That Academy Award win has become both a reference point and a kiss of death. More often than not, *The Broadway Melody* appears near the top of "Worst Best Picture Winners" lists, a status that is both understandable and unjust. As with many Oscar recipients, it's timely entertainment, not timeless art, and as a very early sound film, it now seems as primitive and remote as a relic from the Bronze Age. The dialogue sounds as though they were still trying to figure out exactly how movie talk should sound, the cinematography is static, the musical numbers gauche, if charming, and the dramatics pretty threadbare.

So how, with all these distancing factors, can modern viewers confront such a museum piece? One way comes with perspective. Difficult as it may be, try to imagine how all this looked and sounded to an audience who had never before seen a musical. Next, recall that *Singin' in the Rain*, a musical that truly *is* timeless, is in some ways a tribute to *The Broadway Melody*, using its songs and even some of its technical personnel; think of *Broadway Melody* as sort of a real-life *Dancing Cavalier*, with nobody getting dubbed. Another way comes with a performance that genuinely works. As Hank, Bessie Love is tough, vulnerable, subtle, and touching in a way no one had yet been in sound movies. (Watch Al Jolson in *The Singing Fool* [1928], then look at the scene where Hank breaks down. Case closed.) And, always, there is the history. This is where and how musicals got their start. Without it, there would be no *42nd Street* (1933), no *On*

"The Wedding of the Painted Doll"

Anita Page, Charles King, Bessie Love

Harry Beaumont directs Charles King (center), with Nacio Herb Brown at the piano

the Town (1949), no Cabaret (1972) or Chicago (2002) or La La Land (2016). And, emphatically, no Singin' in the Rain.

Quaint, halting and, for some, impossible, The Broadway Melody needs a willing viewer with an open mind. Put those considerations into play, and it can be seen for what it is: an intrepid, endearing, and necessary cinematic milestone.

Bessie Love, Charles King, Anita Page

WHAT'S MORE

In casting the three leads, MGM astutely covered all the bases. Love was a seasoned movie pro, Anita Page a gorgeous newbie, and Charles King a longtime Broadway veteran. King returned to the stage after a few films, while Love would work steadily over seven decades, from Intolerance (1916) to The Hunger (1983). Page retired in her midtwenties then, in her eighties and nineties, made what can only be called a startling comeback in such epics as, no kidding, The Crawling Brain (2002).

• • •

The technical challenges portrayed in Singin' in the Rain really did happen here. (Lina Lamont's noisy pearls were actually beads on Page's gown.) Normally, the camera was imprisoned in an immobile booth, and in one scene they tried for more mobility with a smaller coffin-like box on wheels. It was moved around by stagehands in stocking feet, and one of them stepped on an exposed carpet tack, screamed, and ruined a take. The tension on the set was never-ending, so much so that one day poor Page became hysterical and had to be sent home.

MUSICALLY SPEAKING

Among many other firsts, this marked the beginning of Arthur Freed's movie career. Years later, still occasionally writing lyrics, he would produce the finest musicals made at MGM, or anywhere else. "The Wedding of the Painted Doll," one of the songs he wrote with Nacio Herb Brown, was shot in early two-color Technicolor. Originally done with live singing and music, it played so inertly on the screen that production head Irving Thalberg ordered a retake. Instead of rehiring the musicians, they used the recording from the first try and thus originated the use of music playback, which is still in use today—although *Les Misérables* (2012) made an awfully big deal of not employing it. "Painted Doll" was long believed to survive only in black and white, but in 2012 a few seconds of its original color were rediscovered—just enough to show why, like the entire film, its initial impact was so huge.

> ### MORE TO SEE
>
> *Gold Diggers of Broadway* (1929): Only about 20 percent of this Technicolor smash hit survives, but it's delightful
>
> *Applause* (1929): Director Rouben Mamoulian reinvents the backstage drama

"The Broadway Melody": Anita Page, Charles King, and Bessie Love front the chorus line.

THE LOVE PARADE

PARAMOUNT, 1929 | BLACK AND WHITE, 107 MINUTES

DIRECTOR AND PRODUCER: ERNST LUBITSCH   SCREENPLAY: ERNEST VAJDA AND GUY BOLTON, BASED ON THE PLAY *LE PRINCE CONSORT* BY LÉON XANROF AND JULES CHANCEL   SONGS: VICTOR SCHERTZINGER (MUSIC) AND CLIFFORD GREY (LYRICS)   STARRING: MAURICE CHEVALIER (COUNT ALFRED RENARD), JEANETTE MACDONALD (QUEEN LOUISE), LUPINO LANE (JACQUES), LILLIAN ROTH (LULU), EUGENE PALLETTE (WAR MINISTER), E. H. CALVERT (AMBASSADOR), LIONEL BELMORE (PRIME MINISTER), BEN TURPIN (LACKEY), YOLA D'AVRIL (PAULETTE), JEAN HARLOW (WOMAN IN THEATER BOX [UNCREDITED])

The government of a mythical kingdom orders a roguish count to woo the country's unmarried queen.

Naughty yet nice, this game changer among early musicals still retains a great deal of its original champagne sparkle. In mid-1929, during the movie musical's chaotic childhood, Ernst Lubitsch decided that there should be a different path. Instead of all the *Broadway Melody* and *Jazz Singer* clones then being made, the master of sophisticated silent comedy created a lavish, stylish operetta filled with witty and clever touches and graced with two brilliant stars. Maurice Chevalier had made a sensational U.S. film debut several months earlier in *Innocents of Paris*, which was good only because of him. Here, with worthy material, he triumphed. So did his costar. Jeanette MacDonald had appeared in a number of Broadway shows, and this would be her spectacular entrance into movies. With the stars' singing and personalities, an elaborate production, a fine score, and ceaseless wit and innuendo, this was one of the year's major successes.

The Love Parade is the first sound film to

Top "Dream Lover": Jeanette MacDonald with ladies-in-waiting (Virginia Bruce, second from left) | **Bottom** Jeanette MacDonald and Maurice Chevalier

approximate the elegance and grace of the silent comedies made by Lubitsch and his many imitators. It also demonstrates the huge strides made by filmmakers in the eight busy months since *The Broadway Melody*. The camera moves fluidly, the actors are at ease with the dialogue, the background scoring is sparkling, and the director is fully in control of the situation from the chic opening credits onward.

How much assurance does Lubitsch have? After Chevalier sings "Paris, Stay the Same," his valet (Lupino Lane) gets a chorus, and another goes to his dog, who barks through the song. This, at a time when many actors were having trouble locating the microphones and speaking their lines. Then there's the way the director is constantly teasing the spectator with all manner of racy possibilities. At one point, as Chevalier begins to tell a risqué anecdote, Lubitsch moves the camera to outside a closed window so he can be seen and not heard, then goes back indoors for a punch line that leaves a viewer to guess how spicy it got in between. Later, Chevalier looks

directly out at the audience to sing "Nobody's Using It Now," making it elegantly obvious that he's bemoaning his sexual frustration. It's clear, too, why MacDonald was considered the "lingerie queen" of early talkies—she sings "Dream Lover" in scanty nightclothes while getting out of bed as a flock of handmaidens provide backup. The other songs are equally adept in connecting the characters and the plot and also the sexual politics—which, it should be remembered, are more of their time than of a later age, and definitely all in fun. Some more prudish viewers, obviously not amused by Lubitsch's approach, wrote to Paramount to complain about it. As it turned out, this was exactly the kind of protest that would lead to the powerful and censorious Motion Picture Production Code.

A few viewers not accustomed to early talkies might find *The Love Parade* a bit stodgy in a few places. More, however, will see exactly why this film was so popular and influential, how advanced it was for its time, and why after many years it continues to be a major treat. Chevalier and MacDonald both went on to more triumphs, as did Lubitsch, yet their work here remains vital, accomplished, and in major ways as fresh as ever.

Paramount Pictures founder and president Adolph Zukor, with director Ernst Lubitsch on the set

WHAT'S MORE

The Love Parade was as much a revelation to people in the movie industry as to the general public. After seeing it, Greta Garbo was so overcome that she walked out of the theater and sat on a curb, silently marveling that, as she put it, "such a film could be made." Then she drove to Lubitsch's house and flung roses at him in ecstatic gratitude. A decade later, director and star teamed to make *Ninotchka*, one of the best films of either's career.

• • •

Maurice Chevalier is perhaps most familiar to audiences for films, like *Gigi* (1958), that he made as a senior citizen. Jeanette MacDonald, for her part, is known far better for her later films with Nelson Eddy, not as a sexy star who runs around in her underwear. Thus, along with its many other virtues, *The Love Parade* is valuable for presenting both stars as audiences first knew them: he as a devastating lady-killer, she as the complete opposite of a buttoned-up prima donna.

MUSICALLY SPEAKING

Victor Schertzinger, who wrote the music, was a composer only some of the time. More often, he was recognized as a major-league film director, with successes like *Redskin* (1929), *One Night of Love* (1934), and *Road to Singapore* (1940). Most of his *Love Parade* songs were too tied to the action to work as stand-alone hits, but the gorgeous "Dream Lover" is an exception. With Schertzinger's sinuous melody and some perilous high notes, it's a fairly difficult song to perform, let alone as well as Jeanette MacDonald did here, live on the set.

> ### MORE TO SEE
>
> *One Hour with You* (1932): Lubitsch and Chevalier, and MacDonald, once again
>
> *Viennese Nights* (1930): Exquisite Technicolor operetta

Left Edgar Norton and Maurice Chevalier | **Right** Jeanette MacDonald and Maurice Chevalier

SUNNY SIDE UP

FOX, 1929 | BLACK AND WHITE, MULTICOLOR SEQUENCE IN SOME PRINTS, 121 MINUTES

DIRECTOR AND PRODUCER: DAVID BUTLER COPRODUCER: B. G. DESYLVA SCREENPLAY: B. G. DESYLVA, LEW BROWN, AND RAY HENDERSON, CONTINUITY BY DAVID BUTLER SONGS: B. G. DESYLVA, LEW BROWN, AND RAY HENDERSON CHOREOGRAPHER: SEYMOUR FELIX STARRING: JANET GAYNOR (MOLLY CARR), CHARLES FARRELL (JACK CROMWELL), MARJORIE WHITE (BEE NICHOLS), EL BRENDEL (ERIC SWENSON), MARY FORBES (MRS. CROMWELL), SHARON LYNN (JANE WORTH), FRANK RICHARDSON (EDDIE RAFFERTY), PETER GAWTHORNE (LAKE THE BUTLER), JACKIE COOPER (JERRY MCGINNIS [UNCREDITED])

To make his fiancée jealous, a Long Island socialite pretends to take up with a working girl.

WILLIAM FOX
Presents
SUNNY SIDE UP
the screens first original all
talking, singing, dancing
musical comedy
With
JANET GAYNOR and
CHARLES FARRELL
SHARON LYNN, FRANK RICHARDSON
EL BRENDEL, MARJORIE WHITE
Original songs, story and
dialog by – DE SYLVA,
BROWN and HENDERSON
Dances staged by SEYMOUR FELIX
Directed by DAVID BUTLER

"An Original Musical Comedy," the on-screen title card announces, and so it is. A sweet love story with dandy songs, this was one of the major hits of its era.

Other movie studios had Jolson or Garbo. Fox Films had Janet Gaynor and Charles Farrell. She was petite and winsome, he was tall and handsome, and they set much of the world on fire in the silent romance *Seventh Heaven*. Neither had much in the way of vocal training, and Farrell's nasally tenor voice seemed at odds with his appearance, but never mind. Their first all-talking picture, Fox decided, would be a musical created by prime Broadway talent. DeSylva, Brown, and Henderson, who created

such hit shows as *Good News*, crafted a slight and engaging story that deliberately strayed from the then-rampant backstage formula. The songs were deftly tailored to the Gaynor-Farrell team's limited vocal range, and Fox's flexible sound equipment made it possible to do more outdoor shooting than was the case at other studios. The result was applauded by critics, who liked Gaynor more than Farrell, and massively embraced by audiences. Although some of the other early Fox musicals were disappointments, this one broke through as one of the year's biggest successes, to be imitated and emulated ad infinitum.

While many early Fox talkies do not survive, this one fortunately does. Yes, it's corny and runs too long, and then there's Farrell's voice and clueless line readings. What's more important is the assurance of the filmmaking, which has little of the stolid quality or timidity that hinders so many 1929 films. It really does act and move like a film, instead of a transplanted stage show, and Gaynor carries the whole thing like a major-league pro. Take a small voice, add a middling-but-spirited affinity for song and dance, and surround the whole of it with a touching kind of sincerity rare in any actor. She *means* this performance, whether doing her hat-and-cane bit in the title song, being optimistic or tearful, or duetting with Farrell on "If I Had a Talking Picture of You." (If ever the early sound era had an anthem, this is it.) When she settles into a comfy chair, pulls out an autoharp, and begins to strum and sing "I'm a Dreamer (Aren't We All?)," a viewer can be momentarily struck by how strange it is, how foreign to later performances and styles. Then, after a few moments, it begins to work: she's looking straight into the camera and out into the audience, she believes every word she's singing, and darned if that authenticity doesn't convince even the unbelievers. Musical film needs sincerity as much as, or more than, it does plush spectacle, big effects, devastating talent. Even this early in the game, an intuitive performer like Janet Gaynor can show what, in a musical, can matter the most.

As with the best and most important musicals, the value of *Sunny Side Up* lies both in its own beguiling self and in its influence. Love stories with songs begin here, and if the path to a *La La Land* is long, it's quite direct. One would never have happened without the other.

"Keep Your Sunny Side Up": Janet Gaynor

WHAT'S MORE

At a time when cameras were mostly nailed down, director David Butler opens this film with a long, roving crane shot of a Manhattan tenement, the camera and microphone picking up tiny vignettes in every apartment window. It works as both a preface for the main action and as a stand-alone virtuoso flourish. It may even seem vaguely familiar: it anticipates the beginning, twenty-five years later, of Alfred Hitchcock's *Rear Window*.

• • •

Janet Gaynor's on-screen sweetness was equaled, off camera, by a sturdy, determined sense of what was and wasn't good for her career. After the triumph of *Sunny Side Up*, Fox immediately dumped her and Farrell into an atrocious musical follow-up called *High Society Blues*. It was, essentially, *Sunny Side Up* without the good parts, and despite its financial success an appalled Gaynor knew that drastic measures were in order. Walking out on her studio and contract, she embarked on a strike for better roles and higher salary. It went on for seven months, a career eternity in 1930. And she won. As director Butler later noted admiringly, Gaynor had guts.

MUSICALLY SPEAKING

While most of the songs in *Sunny Side Up* are staged on a small scale, one doozy of a show-stopper rolls in as part of the big society benefit. As performed by Sharon Lynn and an enthusiastic group of dancers, "Turn on the Heat" is a tribute to love in both the Arctic, with igloos, and the tropics, with bananas. The dance director, Seymour Felix, kindly saw to it that not one phallic allusion would be overlooked, nor one dancer show any inhibition or propriety. What it lacks in taste, it more than makes up for in sheer brass.

MORE TO SEE

Hallelujah! (1929): Director King Vidor's striking semi-musical

Follow Thru (1930): DeSylva, Brown, and Henderson, in lustrous early Technicolor

---

Janet Gaynor and Charles Farrell

"Turn on the Heat"

KING OF JAZZ

UNIVERSAL, 1930, 2016 RESTORATION BY NBCUNIVERSAL | COLOR (TECHNICOLOR), 98 MINUTES

DIRECTOR: **JOHN MURRAY ANDERSON** PRODUCER: **CARL LAEMMLE JR.** SCREENPLAY: **HARRY RUSKIN (COMEDY SKETCHES)** SONGS: **MILTON AGER (MUSIC) AND JACK YELLEN (MUSIC), MABEL WAYNE (ADDITIONAL MUSIC), *RHAPSODY IN BLUE* BY GEORGE GERSHWIN** CHOREOGRAPHER: **RUSSELL MARKERT** STARRING: **PAUL WHITEMAN AND HIS ORCHESTRA, THE RHYTHM BOYS (BING CROSBY, HARRY BARRIS, AL RINKER), CHARLES IRWIN (MASTER OF CEREMONIES), AS THEMSELVES: JOHN BOLES, LAURA LA PLANTE, JEANETTE LOFF, JEANIE LANG, WILLIAM KENT, STANLEY SMITH, THE BRONX SISTERS, GRACE HAYES, THE SISTERS G, GLENN TRYON, MERNA KENNEDY, JACQUES CARTIER, SLIM SUMMERVILLE, WALTER BRENNAN, JACK WHITE, FRANK LESLIE, WILBUR HALL, GEORGE CHILES, MARION STADLER, DON ROSE, AL NORMAN**

Songs, production numbers, and comedy sketches centered around Paul Whiteman and his Orchestra.

Can magnificent sounds and sights compensate for there being no plot? They do here, in a sumptuous riot of music and early Technicolor that had to wait nine decades for its happy ending.

Early musicals are a strange lot, often a world apart from what came later on. Revues, collections of songs and sketches without a story line, offer a case in point. However much they may seem like the opposite of cinema, studios briefly thought that audiences might accept them. They did so with the first one, MGM's *Hollywood Revue*, because of its stars and novelty, and then it was all downhill. By the time of *King of Jazz*, audiences were becoming fed up with musicals in general and revues in particular. Paul Whiteman was a world-renowned bandleader but not a movie name, and the production had been plagued by any number of problems. Besides delays, mismanagement, and artistic uncertainties, it was under the leadership of a director with no prior film experience.

At $2 million, it was one of the most expensive films yet made, and there was little way it could earn back such a cost. The largest financial returns came from nine foreign-language versions released overseas, including one in Hungarian cohosted by Bela Lugosi. It turned up again in 1933 in a much-cut-down version to capitalize on the growing fame of Bing Crosby, who had made his film debut as one of Whiteman's singing Rhythm Boys. For a time it was thought to be lost, then resurfaced in a washed-out video release that looked nothing like the original Technicolor. Finally, in 2016, a major restoration helped *King of Jazz* garner the attention and appreciation it had deserved all along.

Don't expect anything like a conventional musical. Paul Whiteman, famous as he was in the 1920s, is known today mainly by buffs, and what's called "jazz" is far closer to late-1920s pop. It plays like the kind of variety show that long ago was a staple on TV, like Ed Sullivan or *The Hollywood Palace*. A host introduces songs, dances, and comedy, and the ambience is more theatrical than cinematic, with huge sets that

move around far more than the camera does. The early Technicolor is beautiful and also limited, turning *Rhapsody in Blue* into *Symphony in Turquoise*. Sometimes, too, things get surpassingly odd, like the guy who plays "Stars and Stripes Forever" on a bicycle pump. Yet, with all this archaic strangeness, it's beautiful to look at and listen to and even has a kind of formal integrity. Whatever his lack of film experience, director Anderson is quite generous with his bag of tricks, including special effects and the first animated cartoon ever shot in color. The Whiteman

Finale: Nell O'Day and the Tommy Atkins Sextet

Top "Rhapsody in Blue"　|　**Bottom** "Bridal Veil": Stanley Smith and Jeanette Loff, center

musicians play gloriously and there are delightful songs like "Happy Feet," later revived by Kermit the Frog, plus some great eccentric dancers. That *Rhapsody in Blue* centerpiece is fascinatingly over-the-top, and the "Melting Pot" finale can legitimately be termed awe-inspiring.

King of Jazz is both a window onto a lost era and a clear demonstration of why shows like this, and bandleaders such as Whiteman, were so esteemed. Leave the logic for another film, and remember that musicals should, after all, both beguile and impress. Without question, this spectacular production does both those things, and often.

WHAT'S MORE

Aside from Whiteman, the biggest cast name of *King of Jazz* in 1930 was John Boles. He had already starred in the hit movie musicals *The Desert Song* and *Rio Rita*, and here was slated to perform "It Happened in Monterey." Another number, "Song of the Dawn," was intended as a breakout solo for Whiteman singer Bing Crosby . . . at least until Crosby got drunk, crashed his car, and wound up behind bars. An infuriated Whiteman pulled Crosby out of "Dawn" and made it Boles's second number. Crosby was then forced to continue working on *King of Jazz* in the daytime and, every night, be escorted back to jail.

• • •

Although dozens of films, mostly musicals, were shot all or partly in Technicolor in 1929–30, *King of Jazz* is one of the few to survive complete and intact. The early two-color Technicolor process was considered obsolete after the improved three-strip technology arrived in the mid-1930s, and most negatives and prints were junked. Some lost titles survive in black and white, snippets have turned up for several more, and many vanished completely. All the more reason, then, to be grateful for the reemergence of *King of Jazz*, and to hope that more films may be out there awaiting rediscovery.

"It Happened in Monterey": Jeanette Loff and John Boles

Whiteman and his orchestra had been associated with *Rhapsody in Blue* since they premiered the Gershwin piece, with the composer at the piano, in 1924. The film rights to the music alone were an astronomical $50,000, after which Anderson's extravagance took the cost far higher. For the movie's opening engagement, at the Roxy Theater in New York in May 1930, Gershwin was the soloist once again, performing with Whiteman as part of the stage show. In the movie, the pianist is Roy Bargy, who resembled Gershwin enough to sometimes be mistaken for him.

MORE TO SEE

Whoopee! (1930): Eddie Cantor, Technicolor, dances by Busby Berkeley, and a very young Betty Grable

Roman Scandals (1933): More Cantor, more Berkeley, and Lucille Ball's film debut

Paul Whiteman and his Orchestra

LE MILLION

FILMS SONORES TOBIS (FRANCE), 1931 | BLACK AND WHITE, 82 MINUTES

DIRECTOR, PRODUCER, SCREENPLAY, EDITOR, LYRICIST: RENÉ CLAIR   ORIGINAL PLAY: GEORGES BERR AND MARCEL GUILLAMAUD
MUSIC: ARMAND BERNARD, PHILIPPE PARÈS, AND GEORGES VAN PARYS   STARRING: ANNABELLA (BÉATRICE), RENÉ LEFÈVRE
(MICHEL), LOUIS ALLIBERT (PROSPER), PAUL OLLIVIER (GRANPÈRE TULIPE), CONSTANTIN SIROESCO (AMBROSIO SOPRANELLI),
RAYMOND CORDY (LE CHAUFFEUR DE TAXI), VANDA GRÉVILLE (VANDA), ODETTE TALAZAC (LA CANTATRICE)

An impoverished Parisian artist discovers he has won a lottery, and he and his girlfriend scramble to locate the ticket.

America gave birth to the movie musical. Europe was where much of its growing up commenced. Germany, France, and England were the most prominent of the countries with pioneers and artists and innovators, and none was more significant than René Clair. At a time when most American film was literal and prosaic, Clair created *Le million*, a joyfully surreal blend of comedy and music that has been much copied and never duplicated.

In silent films such as *The Italian Straw Hat*, Clair established himself as an artist of extraordinary ingenuity and wit, and he was initially skeptical about adding sound to film. After *The Broadway Melody* helped persuade him of the possibilities, he made *Sous les toits de Paris* (*Under the Rooftops of Paris*). A startling blend of sound and silent movie techniques, it was a bracing departure from more earthbound musicals and a major success. Clair next adapted a stage comedy that had already been filmed in the United States in 1914 as *The Million*, and which in other hands might have been just another backstage musical. Instead, with Clair, *Le million* creates a self-contained, quirky, and marvelously entertaining world in which movement, song, dialogue, and pantomime can intersect and commingle.

Everyone in *Le million* seems to be chasing after something or someone, which makes it fitting that, just like them, Clair pursues every opportunity for visual and musical cues and jokes. Characters pop up constantly to explain themselves musically and move around rhythmically, and one person's conscience even manages to sing a cautionary advisory. A few song sequences appear to start off with more conventional staging—and then Clair moves them in a wildly different path, advancing or commenting on the plot without a pause in momentum. In many scenes, Clair forsakes live sound entirely and uses the music to accompany choreographed melees straight out of a slapstick silent comedy. He punctuates the action with exaggerated sound effects, then goes even further when, to hilarious effect, he overdubs the frenetic action with crowd noises out of a soccer game. Such audacity helped make *Le million* an instant hit in Europe and a major influence on American cinema, where rhymed dialogue, rhythmic movement, and creative sound effects all popped up in musical features and shorts over the next few years. Unfortunately, there would be only one more innovative comedy musical from Clair: the anarchic *À nous la liberté*, in which the frequently cited parallels between him and Chaplin are especially striking. When *Liberté*

"Nous sommes seules": René Lefèvre and Annabella

failed at the box office, he moved permanently to less musical areas.

Clair's meteoric career in musical cinema parallels that of other European filmmakers who found their own ways early on. Among them was England's Victor Saville and, in Germany, Willi Forst, Erik Charell, and Wilhelm Thiele. One of the most arresting works was G. W. Pabst's adaptation of *The Threepenny Opera*. So much creativity and imagination, and then, alas, silence. By the mid-1930s, the equation was playing out in reverse: instead of providing new paths and inspiration for American musicals, those made in Europe shrank into mere imitations of U.S. models, and would remain so until the 1960s. *Le million*, then, is more the central work of a masterful René Clair trilogy than it is a harbinger of great things to come. But what a glorious center it is.

WHAT'S MORE

The opening shot of *Le million* is a spectacular pan over Paris rooftops that deliberately recalls the beginning of its predecessor, *Sous les toits des Paris*. This time, however, it functions as a cheeky in-joke. The men scampering across those rooftops arrive at a skylight and peer in at a group of revelers—who then, for not much reason in particular, proceed to narrate the entire movie as a flashback. Obviously, Clair was not above quoting himself, nor indulging in witty self-parody.

• • •

The lead actress in *Le million*, Annabella, can fairly be described as adorable. Born Suzanne Charpentier, she made her film debut in Abel Gance's *Napoléon* (1927) and, in 1933, again worked productively with René Clair in *Quatorze Juillet*. After more European success, she was signed by Twentieth Century-Fox, who saw her as the French answer to Greta Garbo and Marlene Dietrich. In the end, it was her tempestuous marriage to actor Tyrone Power that drew more attention than her American films, which were less interesting that what she had done in Europe for Clair and others.

Annabella (center)

Though much of its music is fragmented, *Le million* does contain what can be considered a theme song, and naturally Clair finds a clever way to stage it. As a less-than-romantic-looking tenor and soprano sing "Nous sommes seules" ("We Are Alone") onstage, Michel and Béatrice, behind the set, realize that they're still in love. With petals falling and two voices lifted in a lilting waltz, it's one of the best-regarded scenes in the movie, lyrical and captivating and, *bien sûr*, just a little quirky.

> ## MORE TO SEE
>
> *Der blaue Engel* [*The Blue Angel*] (1930): Josef von Sternberg and Marlene Dietrich, searing and sublime
>
> *Sunshine Susie* (1931): The first outstanding British musical, and delightful

René Lefèvre (center)

LOVE ME TONIGHT

PARAMOUNT, 1932 | BLACK AND WHITE, 104 MINUTES (ORIGINAL RUNNING TIME)

DIRECTOR AND PRODUCER: ROUBEN MAMOULIAN   SCREENPLAY: SAMUEL HOFFENSTEIN, GEORGE MARION JR., WALDEMAR YOUNG, BASED ON THE PLAY *LE TAILLEUR AU CHÂTEAU* BY LÉOPOLD MARCHAND AND PAUL ARMONT   SONGS: RICHARD RODGERS (MUSIC) AND LORENZ HART (LYRICS)   STARRING: MAURICE CHEVALIER (MAURICE), JEANETTE MACDONALD (PRINCESS JEANETTE), CHARLIE RUGGLES (VISCOUNT GILBERT DE VARÈZE), CHARLES BUTTERWORTH (COUNT DE SAVIGNAC), MYRNA LOY (COUNTESS VALENTINE), C. AUBREY SMITH (DUKE D'ARTELINES), ELIZABETH PATTERSON (FIRST AUNT), ETHEL GRIFFIES (SECOND AUNT), BLANCHE FRIDERICI (THIRD AUNT), JOSEPH CAWTHORN (DR. DE FONTINAC)

A tailor is mistaken for a nobleman and falls in love with a princess.

History can sometimes make amends after going initially awry. In 1932, *Love Me Tonight* was released to a public far more interested in seeing gangster and sex stories than it was in attending musicals. Now, happily, it is regarded as a masterpiece.

Great films, for the most part, both look back and peer ahead. While *Love Me Tonight* honors such predecessors as *The Love Parade* and *Le million*, it also finds countless ways to advance in new directions. First among its creators is director Rouben Mamoulian, who had already blazed new paths on the stage before turning to film with *Applause* and *Dr. Jekyll and Mr. Hyde*. His mastery is evident as soon as the credits are done, with an opening sequence that has become legendary: as a new day begins, Paris slowly awakens in a riot of sounds, images, and artful cutting. Most films could not improve upon such a scene, yet Mamoulian is just getting started.

In a few minutes, Maurice Chevalier, as a Paris tailor, sings "Isn't It Romantic?" and very quickly that wonderful Rodgers and Hart song is wafting through Paris, into the country and finally to a distant balcony. Jeanette MacDonald, a lovelorn princess, gives it a final chorus, and thus are the two lovers connected before they ever meet. The modern fairy tale that follows is both hilarious and tender, embellished by Mamoulian with unconventional camera angles, musically conceived editing, unexpected sound effects, trick photography, and sly jokes. "Mimi" and "Lover" are among the tunes, and the supporting cast—which sometimes acts as a Greek chorus—includes Myrna Loy as likely the most charming nymphomaniac in movie history. There are mistaken identities, love scenes, reversals of fortune, and a stirringly feminist last-minute rescue by horseback, followed by the happiest of ever-afters.

Because of Chevalier and MacDonald, *Love Me Tonight* is frequently grouped with the films both stars made with director Ernst Lubitsch, which isn't really fair. Where Lubitsch laughs at sex, Mamoulian wholeheartedly embraces the idea of true and sincere love, and his virtuosity even exceeds that of another formative influence, René Clair. In grace and elegance, perhaps the only cinematic equivalents to *Love Me Tonight* may be the best of the Fred Astaire/Ginger Rogers titles, which are vastly different in most ways. Here, the stars don't dance, and don't need to—the director's already done the choreography with the camera and the microphone and the editing, and he's done it brilliantly.

It's something of a wonder that, with all its radiance, this monarch among musicals is less well known than many others of far, far less distinction. For those who haven't seen it, a huge treat lies in store. And, with apologies for stating the obvious, the answer to that lyrical question "Isn't It Romantic?" will always be an emphatic "You better believe it!"

Top Director Rouben Mamoulian and Maurice Chevalier on the set | **Bottom** Myrna Loy, Charles Butterworth, Charles Ruggles, C. Aubrey Smith

"The Poor Apache": Maurice Chevalier

"Mimi": Myrna Loy in a scene later cut from the film

WHAT'S MORE

When Mamoulian signed on to direct, he decided that the script, based on a French play called *The Tailor in the Castle*, required major overhauling. The rewrites pushed back the start of production again and again until finally it collided with Chevalier's upcoming concert tour. Paramount was then forced to pay off the theaters that had booked him. This and other unplanned expenses made it (at $1 million) one of the year's most expensive films. As with *King of Jazz*, it was too costly to earn a profit at a time when musicals were out of favor with the public.

• • •

Like such other major early-1930s films as *King Kong* and *Mata Hari*, *Love Me Tonight* was a victim of the notorious Motion Picture Production Code, which began to monitor movies' content in 1934. When Paramount reissued *Love Me Tonight* in 1949, the Code demanded the deletion of some mildly risqué material, most notably a song performed by Jeanette and her doctor called "A Woman Needs Something Like That." Also missing were references to a local shrine called the Virgin's Spring, plus Myrna Loy singing "Mimi" while wearing a semi-transparent negligee. The only comfort was that, unlike some other Code-slashed titles, the cuts were not done in too jarring a fashion. While *Kong* and some others have been restored, the *Love Me Tonight* footage is still missing and presumed lost. The search for a complete print goes on.

MUSICALLY SPEAKING

Copies of Mamoulian's virtuoso "Isn't It Romantic?" sequence appeared in several subsequent films. The most irreverent one came in the RKO comedy *Diplomaniacs* (1933), with comedian Bert Wheeler in drag as Jeanette MacDonald. Since Paramount owned the rights to the song itself, as well as to "Mimi" and "Lover," all three soon began to turn up as background scoring in the studio's feature films, short subjects, cartoons and, later, television shows. From 1932 to the twenty-first century, those Richard Rodgers melodies have become permanently lodged in the ears and subconscious minds of millions of spectators.

> ### MORE TO SEE
>
> *Sweet Kitty Bellairs* (1930): A nearly forgotten comic operetta gem
>
> *The Cat and the Fiddle* (1934): MacDonald with Ramon Novarro in another sparkling romance

Charles Butterworth and Jeanette MacDonald

42ND STREET

WARNER BROS., 1933 | BLACK AND WHITE, 89 MINUTES

DIRECTOR: **LLOYD BACON**   SCREENPLAY: **RIAN JAMES AND JAMES SEYMOUR, BASED ON THE NOVEL BY BRADFORD ROPES**
SONGS: **HARRY WARREN (MUSIC) AND AL DUBIN (LYRICS)**   MUSICAL NUMBERS: **BUSBY BERKELEY**   STARRING: **WARNER BAXTER (JULIAN MARSH), BEBE DANIELS (DOROTHY BROCK), GEORGE BRENT (PAT DENNING), RUBY KEELER (PEGGY SAWYER), GUY KIBBEE (ABNER DILLON), DICK POWELL (BILLY LAWLER), UNA MERKEL (LORRAINE FLEMING), GINGER ROGERS (ANN "ANYTIME ANNIE" LOWELL), GEORGE E. STONE (ANDY LEE), EDWARD J. NUGENT (TERRY), TOBY WING ("YOUNG AND HEALTHY" GIRL)**

An ailing director struggles to put on a Broadway show despite problems with his star.

"You're going out there a youngster . . . but you've got to come back a star!" This is the definitive backstage musical and, with its fierce energy and Busby Berkeley inventiveness, it remains marvelously fresh many decades later.

If musicals were not completely dead in the dimmest days of the Great Depression, sometimes it was hard to tell. What a master stroke, then, on the part of Warner Bros., to bring musicals back with one that reflected the national mood instead of ignoring it. People in *42nd Street* are destitute, anxious, or both. Director Julian Marsh needs a hit so badly that he ignores his doctor's warnings; star Dorothy Brock tries to keep her career going by playing nice with an investor she loathes; chorus girls Lorraine and "Anytime Annie" make wisecracks and sleep around to get jobs; and young Peggy Sawyer is sweet, talented, and starving. Audiences could identify with this kind of

"42nd Street": Ruby Keeler

desperation, and could then find catharsis when, after Dorothy is injured in a drunken fall, Peggy goes on in her place and triumphs. It didn't matter that Ruby Keeler's acting and singing were appealingly amateurish, and that her tap dancing was more emphatic than graceful. She was someone people could believe in, just as they could believe that the success of her show, *Pretty Lady*, was a harbinger of better times. The musical escapism on view in *42nd Street* is far more hard-edged than it is frivolous, and its final shot is not of Peggy's success but of Marsh standing in an alleyway, exhausted and depleted. In a grim time, song and dance and despair can be a perfect combination.

It was in its musical portions that *42nd Street* racked up the most decisive achievements. The music and lyrics of Harry Warren and Al Dubin were catchy, boisterous, and, for the title song, as driven and riveting as anything in the script. For Busby Berkeley, who had been in Hollywood since *Whoopee!* in 1930, this would be a defining moment. From the outset, his style had strayed visibly from the conventions of filmed song and dance: mass formations that were almost militaristic in their precision, dynamic and sometimes startling camera movements, and that voyeur's appreciation for the faces and figures of beautiful women. His work in *42nd Street* is sometimes conventional ("Shuffle Off to Buffalo") and more

Top to Bottom   Una Merkel, Ruby Keeler, George E. Stone | George Brent, Bebe Daniels, Ruby Keeler, Warner Baxter, George Irving | Una Merkel, Ruby Keeler, George E. Stone, George Brent, Ginger Rogers

often audacious, as in "Young and Healthy" with the camera going overhead to shoot geometrical formations, then coming back down to push its way through a tunnel of chorus girls' legs. Irresistible as they are, Berkeley's numbers can stand alone yet also fit snugly into a production whose concise eighty-nine minutes manage to cover every base.

As with its studio's gangster yarns and low-life sagas, *42nd Street* was made with an eye less toward art than to timeliness and profit. No one envisioned its huge success, let alone that it would revive and reinvent an entire genre, make Busby Berkeley the most imitated director in Hollywood, make stars of Ruby Keeler and Dick Powell, and put Warner Bros. back in the black. All this, essentially, because of one outstanding film, for reasons that are vividly clear every time anyone sees it.

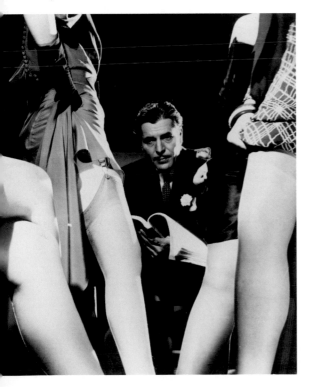

Warner Baxter

WHAT'S MORE

The success of *42nd Street* was in a way as much political as artistic and financial. Unlike other film moguls, the Warners were Democrats, and decided to time the release of *42nd Street* with the incoming presidency of Franklin Roosevelt. The ad campaign borrowed a Roosevelt phrase to herald the film as "A NEW DEAL in Entertainment," and a star-packed train called "The *42nd Street* Special" traveled from city to city for deluxe premieres. The trip culminated in Washington, D.C., on Inauguration Day itself, March 3, 1933, thus creating a synergy that made the new movie seem as fresh and triumphant as the new administration. Both were instant hits, and the entire stunt remains one of the more ingenious and successful promotional campaigns in movie history.

• • •

Although this was Ruby Keeler's feature film debut, she was hardly unknown. She had starred on Broadway in the Gershwins' *Show Girl* and was, famously, Mrs. Al Jolson. Being married to Mr. Show Biz required considerable fortitude, and things grew shaky when, after *42nd Street*, her fame began to exceed his. An ego the size of Jolson's can cast a long, exhausting shadow and, long after the marriage ended, Keeler refused to have her name used in the hit biopic *The Jolson Story*.

MUSICALLY SPEAKING

As the first of the Busby Berkeley Warner Bros. extravaganzas, *42nd Street* shows the dance director in especially good form in the title number. As cued by Warren and Dubin's nervy melody and lyrics, Berkeley presents a bustling and sometimes sordid urban landscape with pushcart vendors, speakeasies, and a phalanx of tap-dancing prostitutes with their johns, as well as an attempted rape that ends in a stabbing. In Berkeley's particular kind of genius, a dark side was definitely part of the whole package.

"Young and Healthy": Busby Berkeley (upper center) lining up an overhead shot of Toby Wing and Dick Powell

MORE TO SEE

Gold Diggers of 1933: More Berkeley, and pure delight

Footlight Parade (1933): Even more Berkeley, and James Cagney, too

On the set. From left: director Lloyd Bacon, George Brent, Warner Baxter, Ned Sparks, Bebe Daniels, Allen Jenkins, Ginger Rogers, Edward J. Nugent, Guy Kibbee, Una Merkel, Ruby Keeler, unknown, cinematographer Sol Polito, Robert McWade, George E. Stone, Dick Powell

TOP HAT

RKO, 1935 | **BLACK AND WHITE, 101 MINUTES**

DIRECTOR: MARK SANDRICH   PRODUCER: PANDRO S. BERMAN   SCREENPLAY: DWIGHT TAYLOR AND ALLAN SCOTT   SONGS: IRVING BERLIN   CHOREOGRAPHERS: FRED ASTAIRE (UNCREDITED) AND HERMES PAN   STARRING: FRED ASTAIRE (JERRY TRAVERS), GINGER ROGERS (DALE TREMONT), EDWARD EVERETT HORTON (HORACE HARDWICK), ALBERTO BEDDINI (ERIK RHODES), HELEN BRODERICK (MADGE HARDWICK), ERIC BLORE (BATES), LUCILLE BALL (FLOWER CLERK [UNCREDITED])

A dancer pursues a model who mistakes him for his none-too-bright producer.

Call him a founding father of the movie musical. Call her one of its most blithe spirits. Fred Astaire and Ginger Rogers are the premiere couple in all of musical film. He was an artist and innovator, she an ideal partner, and their work together couldn't be touched then, let alone now. *Top Hat* finds them at the apex of their art, and if that isn't enough, there's the glorious music of Irving Berlin as well.

They both had ambitious mothers and were in show business from early on. He danced with his sister Adele, she won Charleston contests, and both made it to Broadway. When Adele retired to get married, Fred went out as a single, by which time Ginger was in movies. By 1933, both were under contract to RKO and teamed as the second leads in *Flying Down to Rio*—his second film and her twenty-second. They clicked immediately and were promptly starred in *The Gay Divorcée* (1934), which cemented their partnership and established all its parameters. They would meet, he would chase her, and though not especially interested she would consent to dance with him. While comic supporting players ran interference, the roundelay—and the songs and dances—continued until, finally, they were together for good. This would be the template that saw them through nine films in seven years,

"The Piccolino": Ginger Rogers and Fred Astaire

TH-ADV-38

plus a coda one decade later. Their off screen dynamics are well known: he was tightly focused on dance while she was an all-around talent; he was a driven perfectionist and she sought validation outside the musical realm; they were both strong-willed and resisted the notion that they were "paired," yet were so good together that their partnership had to continue.

Top Hat was their fourth collaboration, and for many their best. Unquestionably, it has the greatest opening of any of their films: a title sequence with his feet dancing onto the screen, then hers, and all the names set in the swankiest deco lettering. He's an American dancer in London, she has the hotel room under his, and their "meet cute" is a classic: when he dances at night, she comes up to complain. The mistaken identity plot follows like clockwork, and under the ultra-smooth direction of Sandrich, it floats along without sagging or bogging down.

"Top Hat, White Tie, and Tails": Fred Astaire

Horton and Broderick and Erik and Eric (Rhodes and Blore) play their prefab roles with spirit and sparkle, plus just enough artificiality to make Fred and Ginger seem more genuine in comparison. At every point, it's as glamorous as those glossy hotel interiors and as confectionary as the soundstage Venice that looks like it just came off a wedding cake. The songs and dances come at regular intervals: his hotel-room solo to "No Strings," their summer-house duet to "Isn't It a Lovely Day (to Be Caught in the Rain)?," the title number, with Astaire mowing down a battalion of top-hatted dancers, the ecstatic "Cheek to Cheek," and the amusing spectacle of the "Piccolino" finale. Musically and choreographically, none resembles the other, and they're all pretty flawless.

Perfectionism such as Astaire practiced is, in fact, the hallmark of *Top Hat*, at least in all ways other than anything seeming mechanical or unfelt. Remember, Astaire and Rogers are divine in large part because, even with all their talent, they're so charmingly, irresistibly human.

Top "Cheek to Cheek": Ginger Rogers and Fred Astaire | **Bottom** Shooting "Cheek to Cheek": Ginger Rogers and Fred Astaire

WHAT'S MORE

Depression-era economics could give films a lot of bang for their budget. *Top Hat* cost just over $609,000, which even at the time was a bargain for a production this size, and it wound up as the second-highest grosser, and biggest profit-earner, of 1935. Astaire and Rogers were that popular.

• • •

Out of all the Astaire-Rogers films, this is the one with the most fabulously unreal art deco-inspired settings: the hotel room with the round bed, the enormous terrace for "Cheek to Cheek," and that fairy-tale Venice. The name of the credited art director, Van Nest Polglase, sounds as out-of-this-world as the sets themselves, so it's tempting to say that he actually designed them. In fact, as the overall head of the RKO art department, he was rarely if ever responsible for any individual project. *Top Hat* was mainly the work of the brilliant Carroll Clark, who much later went to Walt Disney and was partly responsible for the sets in another, far different great musical, *Mary Poppins*.

MUSICALLY SPEAKING

"Cheek to Cheek" is the single most familiar Astaire-Rogers duet for many reasons: the glory of its dancing, the sheer romance that pops off the screen, Rogers's stunning and even notorious feathered gown that visibly sheds, and Max Steiner's sumptuous musical arrangements. Kudos, then, to Astaire and Hermes Pan for the choreography, and to Rogers for those back-bends. None of this, it must be added, would have been possible without some awfully grand starting material. That came from Irving Berlin, in one of his longest, most beautiful, and most complex songs. Here's the kicker: he wrote it, words and music, in just one day.

MORE TO SEE

Flying Down to Rio (1933): Not the standard Fred/Ginger outing, but lots of fun

Gold Diggers of 1935: Busby Berkeley's classic "Lullaby of Broadway"

Director Mark Sandrich and songwriter Irving Berlin on the set

SHOW BOAT

UNIVERSAL, 1936 | BLACK AND WHITE, 113 MINUTES

DIRECTOR: **JAMES WHALE** PRODUCER: **CARL LAEMMLE JR.** SCREENPLAY: **OSCAR HAMMERSTEIN II, BASED ON HIS MUSICAL PLAY,** FROM THE NOVEL BY EDNA FERBER SONGS: **JEROME KERN (MUSIC) AND OSCAR HAMMERSTEIN II (LYRICS)** CHOREOGRAPHER: **LEROY PRINZ** STARRING: **IRENE DUNNE (MAGNOLIA HAWKS), ALLAN JONES (GAYLORD RAVENAL), CHARLES WINNINGER (CAP'N ANDY HAWKS), PAUL ROBESON (JOE), HELEN MORGAN (JULIE LAVERNE), HELEN WESTLEY (PARTHY ANN HAWKS), QUEENIE SMITH (ELLY MAY SHIPLEY), SAMMY WHITE (FRANK SCHULTZ), DONALD COOK (STEVE BAKER), QUEENIE (HATTIE McDANIEL)**

On a Mississippi River show-boat, the captain's daughter falls in love with a gambler.

The first musical play to tackle genuinely big themes and serious situations, *Show Boat* is an authentic landmark. This second of three film versions is a lyrical and deeply felt classic.

Few people in 1927 would have thought of musicalizing Edna Ferber's novel of love and life on the Mississippi. Fortunately, composer Jerome Kern and writer/lyricist Oscar Hammerstein II knew better, and the result was an instant Broadway hit, with more song standards than had ever come out of one show. Since the first film version, in 1929, was an awkward part-silent hybrid, the 1936 remake was a vast improvement. Hammerstein wrote the screenplay and collaborated with Kern on three new songs, and there was a most unexpected choice for director. James Whale was known mainly for

great horror movies—*Frankenstein*, *The Invisible Man*, *Bride of Frankenstein*—and musicals were not his accustomed territory. His *Show Boat*, then, is not a typical Hollywood musical. Instead, it's an intimate epic—a rich and poignant look at the lives, relationships, and customs that will survive and continue over time, and those that will change or pass away. Whale's vision is both theatrical and humanist, giving full sway to both the music and the melodrama with an eye for detail matched by few musicals in any medium.

In addition to superlative material, Whale was blessed with a remarkable group of performers, most of whom had already played their roles onstage. Irene Dunne is a vibrant and affecting (if mature) Magnolia, Allan Jones is sturdy and believable, and Charles Winninger's Cap'n Andy is happily free from excessive shtick. With his two legends, Paul Robeson and the tragic Helen Morgan, Whale is intensely respectful of the power and stature of the former and the wistful fragility of the latter. As sung by Morgan, "Bill" is a heartbreaking showstopper: you know you're witnessing something extraordinary.

Everything works marvelously until right near the end, a place where many productions of *Show Boat* can run off the rails. For all its daring, the show didn't quite have the guts to follow Ferber's book and its less-than-happy ending. Instead, here, there's a dull production number followed by a contrived reunion between the

Top to Bottom | "Bill": Helen Morgan | Irene Dunne, Allan Jones, Charles Winninger, Helen Westley | "Ol' Man River": Paul Robeson

long-separated lovers. Curiously enough, this is one place where the third *Show Boat* film (1951) is more convincing, and that version with its Technicolor pageantry, is, in fact, the preferred *Show Boat* for many viewers. While it lacks the depth and urgency of the earlier film, it does manage to make its final scenes and reconciliation more convincing. Even so, the Whale version contains far too much beauty and majesty to be marred by that one final smudge.

Vital and essential as it is, *Show Boat* is not easy to pull off, not in 1927 and not in the twenty-first century. In its script and its racial sensitivities, in its vocal demands and production values, it can be made to seem quaint, archaic, and false. For the treatment and care it demands and deserves, the right director and cast are crucial. Those circumstances don't happen as often as they should. They certainly do here.

"Can't Help Lovin' That Man": Helen Morgan, Hattie McDaniel, Irene Dunne

WHAT'S MORE

For the venerable Universal Pictures, this film marked the end of an era. The studio had suffered ill financial health for some time, and the high costs of *Show Boat* and another Irene Dunne film, *Magnificent Obsession* (1935), were the last straw for the money people. Shortly before *Show Boat* opened, Universal founder and head Carl Laemmle and his producer son Carl Jr. were forced out and replaced by a new regime with a vastly different (and cheaper) production style. Universal later sold the *Show Boat* rights to MGM for its remake, and instead of circulating a competing product, MGM kept this version on the shelf, unseen, for many years. Even today, it gets less attention than it deserves.

• • •

James Whale's determination to bring his own interpretation to *Show Boat* did not sit well with either Irene Dunne or Allan Jones. Jones, in particular, remained hostile to Whale forever after. "It would have been a much better picture with a different director," he commented late in his life, calling Whale "a very strange man." The director forged a far sturdier bond with Paul Robeson and Hattie McDaniel, whose performances have warmth, humor, and far more dimension than many actors of color were permitted in 1930s Hollywood films.

MUSICALLY SPEAKING

There would be no *Show Boat* without "Ol' Man River" and, as an actor and singer, Paul Robeson was already something of a mythic figure. With his staging, Whale is paying heartfelt tribute to both the song and the performer. The expressionistic vignettes and virtuoso 270-degree camera pan around the singing Robeson manage to be both strikingly stylized and movingly naturalistic. It helps, too, that the song isn't taken at a funereal tempo and, well, keeps rolling along. Between that, the direction, and Robeson's magnificent voice, this is a sequence for the ages.

MORE TO SEE

Music in the Air (1934): Kern/Hammerstein, sung by Gloria Swanson

Roberta (1935): Kern and Dunne and Astaire and Rogers

Paul Robeson and director James Whale on the set

SWING TIME

RKO, 1936 | BLACK AND WHITE, 103 MINUTES

DIRECTOR: GEORGE STEVENS   PRODUCER: PANDRO S. BERMAN   SCREENPLAY: HOWARD LINDSAY AND ALLAN SCOTT, FROM A STORY BY ERWIN S. GELSEY   SONGS: JEROME KERN (MUSIC) AND DOROTHY FIELDS (LYRICS)   CHOREOGRAPHERS: FRED ASTAIRE (UNCREDITED) AND HERMES PAN   STARRING: FRED ASTAIRE (LUCKY GARNETT), GINGER ROGERS (PENNY CARROLL), VICTOR MOORE (POP GARDETTI), HELEN BRODERICK (MABEL ANDERSON), ERIC BLORE (GORDON), BETTY FURNESS (MARGARET WATSON), GEORGES METAXA (RICKY ROMERO), LANDERS STEVENS (JUDGE WATSON)

A hoofer with a gambling problem meets an attractive dance instructor.

In the enchanted stratosphere of films starring Fred Astaire and Ginger Rogers, *Swing Time* takes a place alongside *Top Hat* at the very summit. Many feel it is *the* greatest. The sublime score by Jerome Kern and Dorothy Fields is one of the best that Astaire and Rogers—or anyone—ever had, and then there are those dances.

In *Top Hat*, Astaire and Rogers had cavorted elegantly in a fantasy Venice. In their next film, *Follow the Fleet* (1936), they changed personas and locales, perhaps too drastically, as a sailor on leave and a San Francisco dance-hall entertainer. In *Swing Time*, a happy medium lands them in Depression-era Manhattan with a kind of fanciful reality beyond the usual gossamer threads of mistaken identity and romantic entanglement. He's broke, she teaches dance,

"Waltz in Swing Time" Ginger Rogers and Fred Astaire

and some sly subversion plays on the audience's expectations like a Kern tune on a violin. "The Way You Look Tonight" is one of the greatest ballads ever written, but instead of his singing it to her in an elegant setting, it's in her drab apartment, while she washes her hair. "A Fine Romance" offers sarcasm, not courtship, and in "Never Gonna Dance," Astaire goes so far as to declare a moratorium on the one thing that gives him life and identity. As directed by Stevens, both stars play people we care about, not simply marvel at, and that depth of feeling ingeniously carries forward to the musical numbers.

From *The Gay Divorcée* on, Astaire explored ways in which dance was part of the storytelling, not simply a shiny accessory. *Swing Time* best represents these tendencies and, not coincidentally, finds its dancers in peak form. (Granted,

Astaire's peak form seemed to last for over thirty years.) "Pick Yourself Up" is in the vein of the pair's comic dances and also illuminates the beginning of their relationship. She doesn't know that he's not the gawky non-dancer he pretends to be—until they get out on that floor and the sparks fly. In "Waltz in Swing Time," they're in the big leagues, and this ostensible exhibition piece (with its rousing Kern melody) is also an elated meeting of spirits. "Bojangles of Harlem," will be problematic for many, since Astaire honors the great Bill "Bojangles" Robinson by appearing in dark makeup. Those able to get beyond that will find it an exhilarating tribute from one supreme dancer to another. By the time of "Never Gonna Dance," they've separated, with him vowing that there will never be another dance or another partner. After he

"A Fine Romance": Ginger Rogers and Fred Astaire

movingly sings those sad words, the master stroke comes: their dance and the music reenact the whole affair as we've seen it up to now, with "The Way You Look Tonight" and the "Waltz" recalling their joys and then, with the reprise of "Never Gonna Dance," their parting. At the very end (following that epic group of spins that Rogers did for take after take until her feet bled), she dashes out of the room and out of his life. Even as we know that the happy ending will come, it's heartrending. When, before this, was dance on film allowed to be as moving as any emotional drama?

The star duo did three more films at RKO following this one, and another ten years later at MGM. All have moments of delight and élan, yet cannot approach the achievement of *Swing Time*. Then again, few films can.

Ginger Rogers rehearses with dance director Hermes Pan

WHAT'S MORE

While Astaire and Rogers were both RKO contractees, their workloads differed significantly. Astaire generally did two films per year, each requiring extensive and grueling lead time for him to conceive and plan the dances with co-choreographer Hermes Pan. Rogers, the studio's Jill-of-all-trades, was able to handle every genre and was bounced, constantly, from one film to another. In the years of their main partnership, 1933 through 1939, Astaire made eleven films and she made twenty-eight—doing so, as everyone knows, backward and in heels.

• • •

The career of Betty Furness was far more interesting than her *Swing Time* role as Astaire's snippy fiancée. After dozens of movies, she finally won household recognition on 1950s television by posing next to refrigerators as the spokesperson for Westinghouse appliances. Later, she served with distinction as a consumer advocate, first for President Lyndon Johnson and then for New York State. Woe to anyone seeking to commit consumer fraud when Ms. Furness was on the case.

Helen Broderick, Victor Moore, Fred Astaire, Ginger Rogers

Georges Metaxa, Ginger Rogers, Fred Astaire

MUSICALLY SPEAKING

It takes a while for *Swing Time* to get under-way, but its first song and dance are more than ample reward for a viewer's patience. As if "Pick Yourself Up" weren't dazzling and lively enough as it is, it seems even more dynamic because of the taps that audibly highlight the intricate footwork. Those were mostly recorded separately after the number was shot, on a small section of flooring with an adjacent microphone. Astaire would re-create his taps while he watched the filmed number, and Hermes Pan did the same for Rogers, who usually was busy elsewhere. Essentially, it was like voice dubbing, only in reverse and more strenuous.

MORE TO SEE

The Gay Divorcée (1934): Fred and Ginger's second

Evergreen (1934): English dancing star Jessie Matthews, in her finest film

Fred Astaire and Betty Furness

SNOW WHITE AND THE SEVEN DWARFS

WALT DISNEY, 1937 | COLOR (TECHNICOLOR), 83 MINUTES

SUPERVISING DIRECTOR: DAVID HAND   PRODUCER: WALT DISNEY BASED ON THE STORY BY JACOB AND WILHELM GRIMM
SONGS: FRANK CHURCHILL (MUSIC) AND LARRY MOREY (LYRICS)   CAST VOICES: ADRIANA CASELOTTI (SNOW WHITE), HARRY
STOCKWELL (PRINCE), LUCILLE LA VERNE (QUEEN/WITCH), MORONI OLSON (MAGIC MIRROR), ROY ATWELL (DOC), BILLY GILBERT
(SNEEZY), OTIS HARLAN (HAPPY), PINTO COLVIG (GRUMPY/SLEEPY), SCOTTY MATTRAW (BASHFUL), STUART BUCHANAN
(HUNTSMAN)

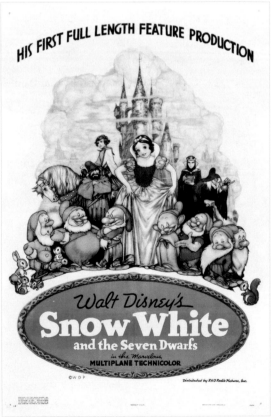

Fleeing the wrath of her jealous stepmother, a princess finds refuge with seven little men.

I t is, as most audiences know a classic and a beloved treasure. Just as important, it's a boldly effective, completely integrated piece of musical cinema.

The first thing to know about this landmark is that it is not, as was long thought, the first animated feature film. A striking German predecessor, *The Adventures of Prince Achmed*, done in silhouette animation, was released in 1926. Nevertheless, *Snow White* was an enormous gamble. Neither Walt Disney nor anyone else was completely certain that audiences would sit through a musical cartoon running eighty-three minutes instead of seven. Could the brightly Technicolored enchantment of animated shorts be sustained over that long a period? Can "real people" be drawn as convincingly as Mickey Mouse or Donald Duck? It's fair to say that Disney and all the artists and technicians who worked on *Snow White* came up with answers that were overwhelmingly in the affirmative. Without *Snow White* and its immense success, there would be no *Pinocchio*, *Fantasia*, *101 Dalmatians*, or *Frozen*. Other animated features have gone beyond *Snow White*'s achievements—*Pinocchio* in technical assurance and emotional depth, *Fantasia* in bold conception, *Sleeping Beauty* in visual splendor—but none quite equal the sum of all its artistic and historical parts. Nor do they match the masterful way that *Snow White* uses music to help cast its spell.

From their very first sound cartoon—*Steamboat Willie* (1928)—onward, Disney and his associates knew that song and melody would be crucial in driving an animated film. First with the likes of *Willie*'s "Turkey in the Straw," later with cribbed classics and new ditties, the Disney cartoons were made of music as much as they were of pen and ink. It was both intuitively smart and immensely savvy to have the songs in *Snow White* define the characters and actions more clearly than almost any other musical film of its time. Except for some Astaire-Rogers outings and a few others, songs and dances generally served to digress from a plot, not advance or deepen it. Contrast this with *Snow White*, which has not been running more than a couple of minutes when the heroine sets everything in motion with "I'm Wishing." In both song and underscoring, the music here always *means* something: making Snow White's forest escape and the Queen-into-Witch transformation more terrifying, wryly noting the Dwarfs' first encounter with soap and, most poignantly, underlining their profound grief when they believe Snow White to be dead. The songs themselves are quite straightforward, befitting

"Heigh-Ho"

the fact that the age of the target audience was judged to be around seven: "Heigh-Ho," let us face it, is not a Gershwin ballad, and the childish quality of Adriana Caselotti's soprano can be startling on a first encounter. Still, the music in *Snow White*, as arranged and presented, is as meaningful and resonant as can be found anywhere in the American musical.

It's easy to praise *Snow White* for its historical status and as a childhood joy, and to dwell on its comedy and drama and, even, real horror. Look and listen past those, then, to the music, which is just as vital and necessary as what is so joyfully seen on the screen. It's a key reason why *Snow White* is as important in the annals of musical cinema as it is to the numberless millions who have loved it for so many decades.

WHAT'S MORE

Disney had not yet begun the practice of crediting performers, so Snow White's vocal artists are not billed on-screen. (Nor is the model for Snow White, who later starred in movie musicals as Marge Champion.) Even without the identification, many of those voices were familiar to audiences in both sound and face, and none more than Lucille La Verne. Loved and feared for her harridan roles in films like *Little Caesar* and *A Tale of Two Cities*, she was versatile enough to provide both the Queen's cultured tones and, indelibly, the Witch's everlastingly fearsome croak.

• • •

As with other early Technicolor films, such as *Gone with the Wind* and *The Wizard of Oz*, *Snow White* has changed its look significantly through the years. In its first release, the color was warm and muted, the better to minimize possible eyestrain. (Remember, these were new trails being blazed here.) Subsequent reissues in theaters and on home video have photographically and digitally manipulated the color into all sorts of permutations, from restrained to candy-box to downright garish. While *Snow White* is eternal, times and tastes and technologies all change.

Walt Disney and the Seven Dwarfs

MUSICALLY SPEAKING

"Whistle While You Work" is both one of *Snow White*'s undoubted highlights and an enormous influence on animated and live-action film, including *Cinderella*, *Enchanted*, and many others. With its bouncy tune, nifty orchestrations, and endless variety of animals-doing-house-cleaning gags, it remains one of the most joyfully kinetic musical numbers ever. A personal favorite among the entire menagerie: the jolly turtle who turns himself into a washboard. Scrubbing laundry seldom (or never) provides this much pleasure.

MORE TO SEE

Pinocchio (1940): Disney's second, and perhaps greatest

Fantasia (1940): Endlessly fascinating, if staggeringly uneven

THE WIZARD OF OZ

MGM, 1939 | **BLACK AND WHITE** (SEPIA)/**COLOR** (TECHNICOLOR), **102 MINUTES**

DIRECTOR: **VICTOR FLEMING** PRODUCER: **MERVYN LEROY** ASSOCIATE PRODUCER: **ARTHUR FREED (UNCREDITED)** SCREENPLAY: **NOEL LANGLEY, FLORENCE RYERSON, AND EDGAR ALLAN WOOLF, BASED ON THE BOOK BY L. FRANK BAUM** SONGS: **HAROLD ARLEN** (MUSIC) AND E. Y. "YIP" HARBURG (LYRICS) CHOREOGRAPHER: **BOBBY CONNOLLY** STARRING: **JUDY GARLAND (DOROTHY GALE), FRANK MORGAN (PROFESSOR MARVEL/THE WIZARD), RAY BOLGER ("HUNK"/THE SCARECROW), BERT LAHR ("ZEKE"/THE COWARDLY LION), JACK HALEY ("HICKORY"/THE TIN MAN), BILLIE BURKE (GLINDA), MARGARET HAMILTON (MISS GULCH/WICKED WITCH OF THE WEST), CHARLIE GRAPEWIN (UNCLE HENRY), CLARA BLANDICK (AUNT EM), TERRY (TOTO)**

A tornado carries a Kansas girl and her dog to a magical, dangerous land.

Is it possible to imagine a world without *The Wizard of Oz*? Without "Over the Rainbow" or the Cowardly Lion or even the Lollipop Guild? Fortunately, such speculation isn't necessary.

As is common with great films, there are always the "what ifs" that might have made it different and less special. Thanks, then, to the producers, artists, and decision-makers at MGM, those who knew that Judy Garland was far more suited to play Dorothy than the better-known Shirley Temple; who realized that Richard Thorpe was not the right director and Victor Fleming was; who decided that Jack Haley would be the Tin Man after Buddy Ebsen became ill from the makeup; and who thought of starting the Technicolor when Dorothy opens the door. Gratitude, also, to Arthur Freed, just before he became a full-fledged producer, for coming up with the idea of hiring E. Y. "Yip" Harburg to write the lyrics, and Harold Arlen to compose the music. In the factory that was MGM, this was clearly an exceptional project, one to draw even finer work than usual. Then, after it began to run on television, new generations changed its status from movie to phenomenon to something greater. No moment of it is unfamiliar, no line unquoted, no performance or scene not beloved. As the on-screen prologue notes, "Time has been powerless to put its kindly philosophy out of fashion." The retreads and deconstructions come and pass; the original always remains.

As with *Snow White*, *Oz*'s magic is so familiar that it's easy to forget how much of it derives from its music and lyrics. The entire Munchkinland sequence—save for the interruption of the Witch—is a self-contained operetta, with songs and recitatives that propel the action and compel Dorothy to get to the Emerald City. The character songs of her three companions, the beguiling "Optimistic Voices," the little makeover episodes of "The Merry Old Land of Oz," and Lahr's peerless "If I Were King of the Forest"—all these are skillful beyond the ways of most musicals. They are accessible to young ears yet, with Harburg and Arlen in charge, supremely witty and sophisticated. As

Judy Garland, Jack Haley, Ray Bolger

for "Over the Rainbow"—could a song be better suited to a film, a situation, and a singer? It's an old legend, and apparently true, that someone in the MGM hierarchy—allegedly, top gun Louis B. Mayer—wanted to cut it. Fortunately for the world, sanity prevailed.

Few musicals of any kind, let alone fantasies, have found such smooth and beguiling ways to connect the songs with the characters and the narrative. While there might have been more music in the last third, it was wise to take out "The Jitterbug," which will likely remain the best-known "cut" song in any movie musical. Surely, with its lively tune and intricate lyrics, it was far too upbeat a piece to be placed at a point in the story when Dorothy and her friends are in grave danger. Perhaps another cut scene, the triumphant reprise of "Ding-Dong! The Witch Is Dead," should have been retained—but, in light of the overall result, that's mere quibbling.

Through artistry, craftsmanship, wisdom, fate, and sheer luck, *The Wizard of Oz* has become a permanent part of millions of lives. Would this be any less so were it not a truly great musical? Take one guess.

WHAT'S MORE

Few movies have been so minutely analyzed and scoured in search of booboos. The most famous one involves Garland's hair, which lengthens and shortens several times during her first scene with the Scarecrow. In another realm entirely is that head-scratcher of an urban myth that holds that someone—usually said to be a Munchkin or a stagehand—committed suicide on the set near the Tin Man's cottage. In reality, the figure moving in the background is not a hanging corpse but actually something quite alive—a sarus crane, rented from the Los Angeles Zoo to provide some exotic set dressing.

• • •

At $2,777,000, *The Wizard of Oz* ranked behind only the original *Ben-Hur* (1925) and *The Good Earth* (1937) as MGM's most expensive production up to that time, and its initial posted loss of $1.15 million was catastrophic. Fortunately, the red ink was erased with reissues in 1949 and, prior to its sale to television, in 1955. Since then the profit has been massive, including home video and an enormously varied amount of merchandising. *Oz* also turns up occasionally in movie theaters, and anyone who's never seen it that way is hereby ordered to do so.

On the set: Ray Bolger, director Victor Fleming, dance director Bobby Connolly, and producer Mervyn LeRoy

MUSICALLY SPEAKING

Judy Garland was always aware of what *The Wizard of Oz* achieved, and what it meant to people. When asked to perform a joking parody of her trademark song on television, she could have not been more adamant. "There will be *no* jokes of any kind about 'Over the Rainbow,'" she declared. "It's kind of . . . sacred. I don't want anybody, *any*where, to lose the thing they have about Dorothy or that song." Not to worry, Ms. Garland. They won't.

"If I Were King of the Forest": Bert Lahr

MORE TO SEE

The Firefly (1937): Jeanette MacDonald in another MGM spectacle

First Love (1939): Probably the finest vehicle for Garland's gifted cohort, Deanna Durbin

---

"Over the Rainbow": Judy Garland

YANKEE DOODLE DANDY

WARNER BROS., 1942 | **BLACK AND WHITE, 126 MINUTES**

DIRECTOR: MICHAEL CURTIZ PRODUCERS: JACK L. WARNER AND HAL B. WALLIS SCREENPLAY: ROBERT BUCKNER AND EDMUND JOSEPH SONGS: GEORGE M. COHAN CHOREOGRAPHERS: LEROY PRINZ AND SEYMOUR FELIX STARRING: JAMES CAGNEY (GEORGE M. COHAN), JOAN LESLIE (MARY), WALTER HUSTON (JERRY COHAN), RICHARD WHORF (SAM HARRIS), IRENE MANNING (FAY TEMPLETON), ROSEMARY DECAMP (NELLIE COHAN), JEANNE CAGNEY (JOSIE COHAN), GEORGE TOBIAS (DIETZ), FRANCES LANGFORD (NORA, SINGER), S. Z. SAKALL (SCHWAB)

Writer/actor/composer/ showman George M. Cohan recalls his career, music, and patriotism.

Biographical stories"—it's a kind of oxymoronic term—have long served as a pretext for musical movies. Few of them are terribly accurate, and although this one is no exception, it's a winner. That is due largely to James Cagney's sensational Oscar-winning portrayal of the multitalented George M. Cohan.

Cohan had been an American institution in the early years of the twentieth century, and became one again after his comeback in the Rodgers and Hart musical comedy *I'd Rather Be Right*. As war clouds began to gather, it was inevitable that there would be a film based on the life of the man who wrote "Over There," "You're a Grand Old Flag," and "Give My Regards to Broadway." Clearly, the Cohan brand of patriotism could rouse the country into coping with another world war, and he was perfectly happy to sell his life story and song catalog to Warner Bros. There was one daunting stipulation: nothing about his personal life would be allowed into the movie ostensibly depicting that life. Cohan the man was not nearly as ingratiating as his songs or professional persona and, dour control freak that he was, he stonewalled any attempt at a coherent biography. Finally, after months of wrangling with screenwriters, he agreed to a relatively accurate retelling of his career coupled with a fictitious version of his second marriage. (No mention of his first marriage, at all.) It looked dubious on paper, it played brilliantly on film, and it became Warner Bros.' biggest success to date.

If *Yankee Doodle Dandy* is a fitting salute to the music (and perhaps the life) of George M. Cohan, it is also a tribute to its star, who inhabits the roles of the on- and offstage Cohan with hearty assurance. All the years of gangster stories, tough melodramas, and occasional comedies made it easy to forget that much of James Cagney's early stage career was spent as a musical performer. His skill in song and dance was as idiosyncratic and magnetic as his acting talent, and he shrewdly modified his own dance ability to reflect Cohan's own distinctive style.

Under the leadership of that master-of-all-genres Michael Curtiz, there is such take-no-prisoners authority at work here that

"You're a Grand Old Flag": Jeanne Cagney, James Cagney, Joan Leslie, Walter Huston, Rosemary DeCamp

resistance seems completely unthinkable. If the plot scenes are not always as stirring as the musical numbers, Cagney makes them more convincing than anyone else could, and even ages believably. Cohan, who died a few months after this film was released, was happy with both the film and Cagney's portrayal—even though he is reported to have commented wryly, after a screening, something on the order of "Nice story. Who was it about?"

The truth of the matter is that *Yankee Doodle Dandy* is as much a celebration of Cagney as it is of Cohan, which makes it a special pity that this masterful performer made so few musicals. He had already had a triumph in *Footlight Parade* (1933), and there would be three more later on; unfortunately, in the best of the trio (*Love Me or Leave Me* [1955]), his duties were strictly dramatic. This, then, is a special pinnacle for Cagney, one where his great gifts make the less appealing truth of the matter seem well and happily beside the point.

WHAT'S MORE

Although Broadway was George M. Cohan's normal habitat, he did appear in a few movies. Three were silent; another a drama, titled *Gambling*, that almost nobody saw; and the fifth was a musical, *The Phantom President* (1932). Cohan stars in a double role as a dull presidential candidate and the charismatic huckster who subs for him. It's funny and fascinating, if not always completely successful. Rodgers and Hart wrote the songs, and in one number Cohan sings, dances, and shows pretty much exactly what he was like as a musical performer. Yes, he does dance something like Cagney. Or, rather, Cagney offers a loving reinterpretation of the original Cohan style.

• • •

Yankee Doodle Dandy is one of those films graced with a perfect final scene: as Cohan walks down the steps of the White House after meeting with President Roosevelt, he suddenly breaks into an ebullient tap dance. Like certain other prime movie moments, that dance was not in the original script. Cagney thought of it a few minutes before shooting started and, without checking with his director, just did it. Curtiz was delighted, just as everyone else has been ever since.

"The Yankee Doodle Boy": James Cagney

MUSICALLY SPEAKING

Most 1940s Hollywood musicals depicting scenes from Broadway shows are woefully inauthentic, most infamously the bogus Warner Bros. "biography" of Cole Porter, *Night and Day*. This, however, is something *Yankee Doodle Dandy* manages to get exactly right. The numbers for the Cohan shows seem pretty good in this regard, and the scene of Cohan in *I'd Rather Be Right* is lovingly accurate in darned near every way. When Cagney-playing-Cohan does the Rodgers/Hart "Off the Record," it's as close to the original show as anyone could possibly get, and a testament to the art of two great entertainers.

MORE TO SEE

Ray (2004): Jamie Foxx as Ray Charles

La Vie en Rose (aka *La môme*) (2007): Marion Cotillard as Édith Piaf

Top "Harrigan": Joan Leslie and James Cagney
| **Bottom** Richard Whorf, James Cagney, Irene Manning

HOLIDAY INN

PARAMOUNT, 1942 | BLACK AND WHITE, 100 MINUTES

DIRECTOR AND PRODUCER: MARK SANDRICH   SCREENPLAY: CLAUDE BINYON, ADAPTATION BY ELMER RICE FROM AN IDEA BY IRVING BERLIN   SONGS: IRVING BERLIN   CHOREOGRAPHERS: FRED ASTAIRE (UNCREDITED) AND DANNY DARE STARRING: BING CROSBY (JIM HARDY), FRED ASTAIRE (TED HANOVER), MARJORIE REYNOLDS (LINDA MASON), VIRGINIA DALE (LILA DIXON), WALTER ABEL (DANNY REED), LOUISE BEAVERS (MAMIE), IRVING BACON (GUS), MAREK WINDHEIM (FRANÇOIS), BOB CROSBY'S BAND (ORCHESTRA)

Romance and rivalry at a Connecticut inn open only on holidays.

It's best known for giving the world "White Christmas," and some confuse it with the 1954 film of that title. It deserves a better fate, and more recognition. With Crosby's singing, Astaire's dancing, and Berlin's songs, it's a joyous entertainment.

While also writing other scores for movies and shows, Irving Berlin became the master of a very particular type of musical: a "catalog" filled to the brim with a mix of new and old tunes in a direct predecessor of films like *An American in Paris* and more recent jukebox shows such as *Jersey Boys*. In films such as *Alexander's Ragtime Band, Blue Skies, Easter Parade*, and *There's No Business Like Show Business*, the scripts were rarely more than excuses for Berlin's songs, which came around like lilting clockwork.

MUST-SEE MUSICALS

74

"Let's Say It with Firecrackers": Fred Astaire

Marjorie Reynolds and Fred Astaire

Holiday Inn is the best of the Berlin catalog musicals, with a catchy premise and, especially, two high-powered stars performing outstanding material. Crosby is appealingly laid-back and in stupendous voice, and Astaire offers brilliant dancing while playing a more devious character than usual. Although their two female partners are perfectly adequate, they definitely take a back seat to the gentlemen. (Mary Martin, the original choice for Linda, had to bow out due to pregnancy.) The songs, needless to say, are better than the script, and whenever things begin to congeal, there's always another number coming up, sung or danced with Old Master virtuosity. There is also slick and smart direction by Mark Sandrich, who had already worked with Astaire on five of his eight films with Ginger Rogers.

The format of *Holiday Inn*'s plot ensures that most of Berlin's songs are connected with one holiday or another. Most famous, of course, is "White Christmas," an immediate hit in 1942 and forever after. It had not been tagged as the movie's main song, not by Berlin or Crosby or anyone else; that distinction was to have gone to "Be Careful, It's My Heart," at least until war was declared right in the middle of shooting. Suddenly, a song suffused with cozy nostalgia for a peaceful holiday, heard in Bing Crosby's warm and reassuring tones, seemed urgent and necessary. The abrupt switch to wartime was also partly responsible for giving Astaire the most literally explosive solo of his entire career. As the script would have it, the "Let's Say It with Firecrackers" dance is pure improvisation, Astaire finding himself without a partner and making it up as he goes along with the help of a lit cigarette and a bunch of fireworks. As with a few other classic Astaire solos, there's some obvious gimmickry at work here . . . and who would have it any other way?

Crosby and Astaire reteamed four years later for another Berlin songfest, *Blue Skies*. Unfortunately, this occasion was marred by an unpleasant script and notably less charm. Nor, despite its status as a seasonal perennial, can *White Christmas* truly hold a Christmas candle to *Holiday Inn*, which remains a year-round pleasure.

Left Bing Crosby, Virginia Dale, Marjorie Reynolds, Fred Astaire |
Right Fred Astaire, Bing Crosby, Walter Abel

WHAT'S MORE

Holiday Inn is one of several beloved "Christmas movies" that did not originally open during the holiday season. It opened in the dead of summer (August), as did *Christmas in Connecticut* (1945). *Remember the Night* overshot the holiday by opening in January 1940, *It Happened on Fifth Avenue* was first shown in April 1947, and *It's a Wonderful Life* was not widely seen until January and February 1947. A couple of months later, in June 1947, there arrived the all-time favorite Santa story on film, *Miracle on 34th Street*. Obviously, studios felt that a seasonal tie-in was not a built-in guarantee of success, whereas today a seasonal release date would be locked in even before the film was produced, or possibly even written.

• • •

What's up with the animated turkey on the calendar hopping between the third and fourth Thursday in November? In 1942, few would have had to ask. In 1939, President Roosevelt attempted to boost the economy by moving Thanksgiving a week earlier, allowing for a lengthier Christmas shopping season. The resulting controversy was extremely partisan and not settled until 1941, when the fourth Thursday of November became, officially, Thanksgiving Day. Though the movie doesn't say it, the whole affair was widely known as "Franksgiving."

MUSICALLY SPEAKING

Holiday Inn is full to overflowing with all manner of dandy seasonal songs, plus one that poses some major problems. "Abraham," Berlin's tribute to the sixteenth president, features Crosby, Reynolds, and chorus extolling Mr. Lincoln at length while wearing the dark makeup known as blackface. Though it makes a plot point—Crosby is trying to conceal Reynolds's identity from Astaire—it now makes for highly uncomfortable viewing. Many recent cable television airings of *Holiday Inn* have removed it entirely, which is an understandable, if questionable, way to deal with the situation. Numbers of this sort were present in movie musicals from the beginning and started to taper off in the 1940s until, around 1953, they were gone entirely. Times change, and so does entertainment.

> ### MORE TO SEE
>
> *Alexander's Ragtime Band* (1938): Another Berlin cavalcade
>
> *Springtime in the Rockies* (1942): Wartime escapism with Betty Grable and Carmen Miranda

Bing Crosby and Marjorie Reynolds

CABIN IN THE SKY

MGM, 1943 | BLACK AND WHITE, 98 MINUTES

DIRECTOR: VINCENTE MINNELLI PRODUCER: ARTHUR FREED SCREENPLAY: JOSEPH SCHRANK, BASED ON THE MUSICAL PLAY BY LYNN ROOT SONGS: VERNON DUKE (MUSIC) AND JOHN LA TOUCHE (LYRICS), HAROLD ARLEN (MUSIC) AND E. Y. "YIP" HARBURG (LYRICS) CHOREOGRAPHER: ARCHIE SAVAGE (UNCREDITED) STARRING: ETHEL WATERS (PETUNIA JACKSON), EDDIE "ROCHESTER" ANDERSON (LITTLE JOE JACKSON), LENA HORNE (GEORGIA BROWN), LOUIS ARMSTRONG (THE TRUMPETER), REX INGRAM (LUCIUS/LUCIFER JR.), KENNETH SPENCER (REVEREND GREEN/THE GENERAL), [JOHN W.] "BUBBLES" (DOMINO JOHNSON), OSCAR POLK (THE DEACON/FLEETFOOT), MANTAN MORELAND (FIRST IDEA MAN), BUTTERFLY MCQUEEN (LILY)

Heaven battles hell for the soul of a gambling man with a loving and devout wife.

I f the eternal struggle between good and evil sounds like somber subject matter for a musical, think again. Across many decades of changing tastes and attitudes, *Cabin in the Sky* continues to endure and delight.

It was rare, in the 1940s, for a Broadway show to feature an entirely African American cast, and nearly unheard-of for that show to become a movie. On the stage, *Cabin* had attracted rave reviews and only mild success, and MGM's Arthur Freed assigned this rather iffy project to Vincente Minnelli, who had next to no film experience. Fortunately, Minnelli demonstrated his musical bona fides almost immediately, and he was aided immeasurably by a once-in-a-lifetime cast. Ethel Waters re-creates her stage

role, with Eddie "Rochester" Anderson as her backsliding husband and the luscious young Lena Horne as the devil's go-to temptress. (It's one of the few times Hollywood gave Horne an actual role, instead of a singing bit that could be removed if it offended white audiences in certain theaters across the country.) Also present is the formidable Rex Ingram, who had played God ("De Lawd") in *The Green Pastures* and here switches to the other side as Lucifer Jr. Butterfly McQueen, Prissy in *Gone with the Wind*, is Petunia's friend Lily, and Louis Armstrong and Duke Ellington turn up in cameo appearances. Although George Balanchine had been the choreographer for the show, most of its dancing was left behind.

Another change came when, as with *The Wizard of Oz*, a supposedly "real" fantasy was made to have been only a dream. A few of the original songs were replaced and, while new songs added to a movie version tend to be inferior and forgettable, *Cabin* contains the gorgeous exception: Harold Arlen and Yip Harburg's "Happiness Is Just a Thing Called Joe," sung unforgettably by Waters.

There are parts of *Cabin in the Sky*, it must be said, that can make today's viewers uncomfortable or even angry. That "tale of faith" foreword is condescending, the emphasis on gambling is unfortunate, and some stereotypes here and there are odious, if far less so than in a number of other films and television shows. Fortunately, little of this detracts from the overall effectiveness of the production and the performances. Much of that is due to the sensitivity of Minnelli, whose gift for creating interesting visuals also extends to his treatment of the cast. Rejecting some of the decor originally

[John W.] "Bubbles", Ethel Waters, Ernest Anderson, Eddie Anderson, Lena Horne

planned for Petunia's house, he observed that inexpensive furniture need not be rundown—a small but telling sign of respect for both the characters and the actors. He took special pains in working with Ethel Waters, who gives one of the great performances in all musical film. Both her acting and singing have a kind of majestic warmth and sincerity, and she even adds some high-kicking dance steps. Eddie Anderson, with his distinctively hoarse voice, makes a fine partner, and Horne's Georgia, more kittenish than wicked, is altogether irresistible.

Shortly after Lena Horne played Georgia Brown, MGM loaned her to Twentieth Century-Fox to star in another all-star, all-black musical. *Stormy Weather* (1943) may even exceed *Cabin in the Sky* with its roster of virtuoso performers, as well as Horne's classic rendition of the title song. Where it falls short is in its humdrum script and direction, and therein lies the difference between an uneven film with fabulous parts and a superior one that diverts and enthralls all the way through. Then and now, *Cabin in the Sky* is victorious, and altogether wonderful.

Eddie Anderson, Ethel Waters, Kenneth Spencer

Butterfly McQueen, Kenneth Spencer, Ethel Waters, Clinton Rosemond, Eddie Anderson

WHAT'S MORE

The faith Ethel Waters shows as Petunia was hers offscreen as well, which makes her performance all the more luminous and authentic. It was, however, coupled with a reputation for being difficult, hostile, and paranoid. While shooting "Honey in the Honeycomb," Waters grew to believe that Minnelli and the crew were favoring Lena Horne at her expense. Her reaction was an on-the-set blowup that was, in Horne's words, "an all-encompassing outburst, touching everyone and everything that got in its way." So mighty and terrible was her eruption that shooting was suspended for the rest of the day, and after this the film's subsequent tornado seemed almost feeble in comparison.

• • •

Speaking of that tornado: if it seems familiar, it should. Given *Cabin*'s restricted budget, for that big blow it was necessary to resort to using stock footage left over from *The Wizard of Oz*. It must be wondered if audiences back then recognized it as much as they do now.

Top to Bottom   "Life's Full O' Consequence": Eddie Anderson and Lena Horne | Louis Armstrong, Rex Ingram, Mantan Moreland | Ethel Waters, Duke Ellington, director Vincente Minnelli on the set

MUSICALLY SPEAKING

Viewers are generally disappointed that Louis Armstrong is on-screen only briefly, with just one short trumpet solo. Originally, he had considerably more to do, with an Arlen/Harburg song called "Ain't It the Truth" staged as a big-scale production number set in hell. There then followed a literally bubbly reprise by Lena Horne, seated in her bathtub. Eventually the entire sequence was removed, probably for being too long and, with Horne, repetitive. The film of Armstrong's portion is lost, while some of Horne's survives—and, predictably, is enchanting.

MORE TO SEE

Stormy Weather (1943): Lena Horne and Fats Waller are only two of the many stars seen here at their peak

The Gang's All Here (1943) Wartime escapism, via Busby Berkeley

At last on the screen!

CABIN IN THE SKY

What a Cast!
* **ETHEL WATERS**
* *Eddie* **"ROCHESTER"** *Anderson*
* **LENA HORNE**
* **Louis Armstrong** * **Rex Ingram**
* **Duke Ellington & His Orchestra**
* **The Hall Johnson Choir**

A
Metro-
Goldwyn-
Mayer
PICTURE

Artwork by Al Hirschfeld

COVER GIRL

COLUMBIA, 1944 | COLOR (TECHNICOLOR), 107 MINUTES

DIRECTOR: **CHARLES VIDOR**   PRODUCER: **ARTHUR SCHWARTZ**   SCREENPLAY: **VIRGINIA VAN UPP, ADAPTED BY MARION PARSONNET AND PAUL GANGELIN FROM A STORY BY ERWIN S. GELSEY**   SONGS: **JEROME KERN (MUSIC) AND IRA GERSHWIN (LYRICS)**   CHOREOGRAPHERS: **VAL RASET, SEYMOUR FELIX, GENE KELLY (UNCREDITED), AND STANLEY DONEN (UNCREDITED)**   STARRING: **RITA HAYWORTH (RUSTY PARKER/MARIBELLE HICKS), GENE KELLY (DANNY McGUIRE), LEE BOWMAN (NOEL WHEATON), PHIL SILVERS (GENIUS), LESLIE BROOKS (MAURINE MARTIN), EVE ARDEN (CORNELIA "STONEWALL" JACKSON), JINX FALKENBURG (HERSELF), OTTO KRUGER (JOHN COUDAIR), JESS BARKER (COUDAIR AS A YOUNG MAN), ANITA COLBY (MISS COLBY)**

When a dancer wins a contest to become a cover girl, she jeopardizes her relationship with her club-owner boyfriend.

Technicolor musicals were surefire money-earners during World War II, expensive to make yet returning a major profit. If the music, dance, and lush production were important, the presence of beautiful women was seen by studios as irresistible incentive for keeping up morale and moving toward victory. In addition to being the ultimate wartime celebration of female beauty, *Cover Girl* is, in unexpected ways, quite an innovative piece of cinema.

Cover Girl was Columbia Pictures' most ambitious project since the departure of director

Frank Capra, whose Oscar-winning films were responsible for putting the studio into the major leagues. Under the legendarily dictatorial

"Long Ago and Far Away": Gene Kelly and Rita Hayworth

Rita Hayworth

Harry Cohn, Columbia was smaller and more tightly organized than other studios, lacking the resources-at-the-ready production mechanism of Fox or MGM. It did, however, have a newly emergent star, and even in the era of Hedy Lamarr and Lana Turner, Rita Hayworth was spectacular. Her face, in close-up, was perfect, her dancer's body moved with ineffable grace, and she possessed what may have been the world's best hair. (Her trademark auburn was not its original color, as if that mattered.) There was also something soulful about Hayworth that set her apart, in and out of musicals. Where Betty Grable was cheerfully "this is me," everything present and evident, Hayworth could seem a little remote, her scorch tempered by a private sensitivity. She seemed happiest on-screen while dancing, and after she fared well opposite Fred Astaire, her studio teamed her with Gene Kelly, whose movie career was just gaining momentum. In drama as well as dance, the pairing worked, and still works, extremely well. His smart-guy attitude balances her sweetness, and their respective kinds of physicality give them an erotic charge that earlier musicals rarely delivered.

For an outsized production such as *Cover Girl*, it would be necessary for Columbia to assemble a big show out of smaller parts—three costume designers, for example, when one would generally be the norm, and multiple choreographers. Though neither Kelly nor his young colleague Stanley Donen was given on-screen credit, their work on *Cover Girl* was recognized as a leading cause of its success. The theatrical numbers in the film work well enough, in a standard Fox-backstage-musical

kind of way, while those done by and with Kelly advance the plot and deepen the characters. In "Make Way for Tomorrow," the energy and optimism seem almost limitless, and "Long Ago and Far Away" is as graceful a duet as those by Astaire with Rogers. Most sensationally, there is the "Alter Ego" ballet, which features Kelly vs. Kelly—Danny McGuire's romantic and professional conflicts duking it out in a frenzied duet on a deserted street. It remains one of the greatest of Kelly's dances.

With all its loving craftsmanship, *Cover Girl* is not consistently the sum of its brilliant parts, or its brilliant stars. The screenplay, in particular, appears to lack the last degree of polish of the cast, songs, and production. This seems to be an occasional flaw with Columbia's "A" films, though fortunately in this case the glitches serve to make the best parts seem that much more luminous. A milestone in Kelly's career, *Cover Girl*, with *Gilda* (1946), was also the apotheosis of the love goddess known as Rita Hayworth. Most musicals get by with far, far less.

Rita Hayworth and Eve Arden

Top Gene Kelly and Rita Hayworth | **Bottom** "Who's Complaining?":
Leslie Brooks, Phil Silvers, Rita Hayworth (center)

WHAT'S MORE

If Hayworth looks even more radiant than usual, much of the glow came from being in love. She married Orson Welles on September 7, 1943, midway through filming. It made her less happy, here and elsewhere, that she was not given the opportunity to do her own singing. She did, in fact, have a pleasant voice, as she proved in some TV appearances later on. For *Cover Girl*, the vocal honors went to the uncrowned queen of Hollywood dubbers, Martha Mears. Ms. Mears had already performed "White Christmas" in *Holiday Inn*, she would dub Hayworth again in *Tonight and Every Night*, and literally dozens of films would feature her plush, if necessarily anonymous, vocal stylings.

• • •

The five-foot-six Hayworth had to wear lower heels when she played opposite Astaire, and would need to do so again with the five-foot-eight Kelly. Harry Cohn initially thought Kelly too tough-looking for a romantic leading man, and it took some argument to convince him otherwise. As Kelly later recalled of the battle with Cohn, "It was like Gandhi against the British Empire. And we know who won."

MUSICALLY SPEAKING

The hit song of *Cover Girl*, "Long Ago and Far Away," also serves as underscoring for that superb "Alter Ego" dance where, strikingly, Kern's beautiful melody is twisted around to fit Kelly's dancing and the dark emotional underpinnings of the number. If Astaire could get deep, too, this is more fraught and neurotic, befitting Kelly's earthier persona—almost as if film noir was being set to music.

MORE TO SEE

For Me and My Gal (1942): Gene Kelly's debut, alongside Judy Garland

Ziegfeld Girl (1941): Garland, Hedy Lamarr, and Lana Turner, with backstage drama and Busby Berkeley spectacle

"Make Way for Tomorrow": Phil Silvers, Rita Hayworth, Gene Kelly

MEET ME IN ST. LOUIS

MGM, 1944 | COLOR (TECHNICOLOR), 113 MINUTES

DIRECTOR: VINCENTE MINNELLI   PRODUCER: ARTHUR FREED   SCREENPLAY: IRVING BRECHER AND FRED F. FINKLEHOFFE, BASED ON THE *NEW YORKER* STORIES AND SUBSEQUENT BOOK BY SALLY BENSON   SONGS: RALPH BLANE (MUSIC) AND HUGH MARTIN (LYRICS)   CHOREOGRAPHER: CHARLES WALTERS   STARRING: JUDY GARLAND (ESTHER SMITH), MARGARET O'BRIEN ("TOOTIE" SMITH), MARY ASTOR (MRS. ANNA SMITH), LUCILLE BREMER (ROSE SMITH), LEON AMES (MR. ALONZO SMITH), TOM DRAKE (JOHN TRUETT), MARJORIE MAIN (KATIE), HARRY DAVENPORT (GRANDPA), JOAN CARROLL (AGNES SMITH), JUNE LOCKHART (LUCILLE BALLARD)

In the months leading up to the 1904 World's Fair, a St. Louis family must confront the possibility of change and upheaval.

Not all classic musicals retain their initial luster. Some, finally seen after long anticipation, don't live up to their reputation; others, when revisited, expose their tricks and flaws. Then there is *Meet Me in St. Louis*. It never disappoints, it stays fresh, and it's one of the best musicals, and films about families, ever made.

In an era of brassy backstage entertainments, *Meet Me in St. Louis* found a new path for musicals: graceful, meticulous, character-driven, orderly on the surface yet deeply felt—all, moreover, without a conventional plot. In *Cabin in the Sky*, Vincente Minnelli departed from most musical norms with fresh subject matter and extraordinary attention to detail. In *St. Louis*, he went even further, transforming material that in other hands would have been a bogus, saccharine story. It's as if it truly is taking place in 1904—the decor, the protocols of running a household and operating as a family, the social structures and comforts and fears all seem to float organically. Even with a formidable star presence in Judy Garland and a gorgeous group of songs by Hugh Martin and Ralph Blane, everything is balanced and connected. The music flows logically through the action, the Smith family members do seem related, and the Smith house is such a powerful presence that, without question, it's one of the main characters. A way of life is being portrayed, and the

emotional charge is as strong now as when, in 1944, wartime audiences were being threatened with their own kind of upheaval.

Garland, who originally did not want to play a lovelorn teenager, quickly responded to both the director (whom she later married) and the material in a glowing fashion. So did Margaret O'Brien, whose biggest scenes— Tootie's Halloween and her destruction of the snow people after "Have Yourself a Merry Little Christmas"—evoke childhood's joys and terrors in a way matched by few other films. Again, it is the guidance of Minnelli that points the way, just as it does with all the little touches that make the Smiths so particular: Grandpa's hat collection, Agnes wearing Papa's old shoes, Tootie's doll cemetery, and more. One scene can stand as a representative of the overall quality. The father's

Margaret O'Brien and Judy Garland

announcement of the impending move to New York is greeted by consternation, even anger, and the family practically shuts down. Then the wise mother goes to the piano. She and Papa sing "their" song, everyone troops back into the parlor, and there is a kind of healing. With its strong yet contained feelings, its sense of bonds being frayed but not torn, this scene offers depth and insight such as "classic Hollywood" seldom delivers. The marvel of the film is that it scales these heights repeatedly, even constantly.

The script of *Meet Me in St. Louis* is so strong and well-crafted that it could have stood alone as a non-musical, a warm and amusing series of family reminiscences with a little crisis tossed in. Yet, happily, it's a musical, a great one that perhaps is even more blissful and beautiful now than when it was new.

Top to Bottom Judy Garland and Lucille Bremer | Judy Garland and Tom Drake | "You and I": Ma[ry] Astor and Leon Ames | Left "Boys and Girls Li[ke] You and Me": Tom Drake and Judy Garland in th[e] scene and song later cut from the film

WHAT'S MORE

In 1928, Arthur Freed had been the lyricist half of MGM's first songwriting duo, alongside composer Nacio Herb Brown. For *Meet Me in St. Louis*, the pair teamed up again to write "You and I," sung by the Smith parents after the announcement of the family's impending move. Not content to simply write the lyric (and produce the film), Freed also supplied the singing voice for Leon Ames, as Papa.

• • •

A film as successful as this one (the greatest profit to date for an MGM musical) will naturally spawn imitations, in this case a procession of nostalgia-drenched family tales forged from a similar template: *Summer Holiday, Isn't It Romantic?, On Moonlight Bay*, and numerous others. The closest copy was *Centennial Summer* (1946), which featured the final score by Jerome Kern and appropriated another American world's fair (in 1876) for its setting. Pretty and tuneful, it was also—as directed by Otto Preminger—so joyless as to be a catalog of all the mistakes that *St. Louis* happily avoided.

MORE TO SEE

High, Wide, and Handsome (1937): Another innovative director, Rouben Mamoulian, and Jerome Kern songs

Ziegfeld Follies (1945): Plotless and sometimes glorious revue, mainly directed by Minnelli, with Garland, Astaire, Kelly, and more

---

MUSICALLY SPEAKING

The main songs were by Hugh Martin and Ralph Blane, a few were old standards, and one was by Brown/Freed. Another, the work of Rodgers and Hammerstein, wound up on the cutting room floor. Originally, Judy Garland sang "Boys and Girls Like You and Me" to Tom Drake as they walked around the fair's construction site, shortly after "The Trolley Song." (Garland's rendition survives in audio recordings.) The song had already been dropped from *Oklahoma!* during tryouts, and would be cut yet again when Frank Sinatra sang it in MGM's *Take Me Out to the Ball Game*. While it's since turned up as both a vocal and instrumental in various productions of Rodgers and Hammerstein's *Cinderella*, it does seem to be somewhat jinxed.

On the set: director Vincente Minnelli, Joan Carroll, Margaret O'Brien

ON THE TOWN

MGM, 1949 | COLOR (TECHNICOLOR), 98 MINUTES

DIRECTORS AND CHOREOGRAPHERS: **STANLEY DONEN AND GENE KELLY** PRODUCER: **ARTHUR FREED** SCREENPLAY: **BETTY COMDEN AND ADOLPH GREEN, BASED ON THEIR MUSICAL PLAY** SONGS: **LEONARD BERNSTEIN (MUSIC), ROGER EDENS (MUSIC), AND BETTY COMDEN AND ADOLPH GREEN (LYRICS)** STARRING: **GENE KELLY (GABEY), FRANK SINATRA (CHIP), BETTY GARRETT (BRUNHILDE "HILDY" ESTERHAZY), ANN MILLER (CLAIRE HUDDESON), JULES MUNSHIN (OZZIE), VERA-ELLEN (IVY SMITH), FLORENCE BATES (MADAME DILYOVSKA), ALICE PEARCE (LUCY SHMEELER), GEORGE MEADER (PROFESSOR)**

Three sailors find love during a hectic twenty-four-hour leave in Manhattan.

Exuberant and significant and joyful, *On the Town* forms a dynamic bridge between two eras of moviemaking. The older-style studio-bound musicals, with their backstage plots, choruses, and specialty artists had been successful for a long time. In *On the Town*, the genre began to explore different, often innovative ways: shooting outside the studio, less formulaic scripts, allowing dance to propel the plot instead of diverting from it. There had, of course, been all sorts of predecessors, and it must be said that *On the Town* occasionally carries a whiff of older styles. Nevertheless, it remains a true groundbreaker, a dazzling tour of New York which seldom flags and never disappoints. This is all fortunate, since *On the Town* is also a blatant example of a time-dishonored movie trope: a hit show making it onto film with nearly all its original songs replaced by new ones that aren't as memorable. This change was made at the behest

Top Vera-Ellen, Gene Kelly, Ann Miller, Jules Munshin, Frank Sinatra, Betty Garrett
Bottom Gene Kelly (with Vera-Ellen)

of producer Arthur Freed, who disliked the original Leonard Bernstein songs and thought them too complex for movie audiences. Only three were retained, plus some ballet music, and in came new songs with music by MGM's Roger Edens and lyrics by Betty Comden and Adolph Green.

Gene Kelly and Stanley Donen, directing their first film, wanted to follow the new postwar trend toward location shooting and do the entire picture in New York. This was judged technically and financially impossible, so as a compromise they shot the indoor scenes in California, then the exteriors in New York. It wasn't, as has been claimed, the first movie musical filmed on location, since musicals had been doing that since 1929. It was, however, the first one to make extensive use of New York locations. Between crowd control, cloud control, and music playback, the Manhattan/Brooklyn shoot was a logistical nightmare, and in the finished film (notably around Rockefeller Center) eager flocks of civilian spectators can be glimpsed standing behind studio barricades.

It's not simply the use of real locations that gives *On the Town* its special zip. Whether or not Donen and Kelly were deliberately trying to take the musical in a different direction, their instincts constantly led them down new paths. Contrast their work with the previous Kelly/

Top to Bottom | "Prehistoric Man": Gene Kelly, Frank Sinatra, Ann Miller, Jules Munshin, Betty Garrett | "On the Town": Betty Garrett, Frank Sinatra, Ann Miller, Jules Munshin, Vera-Ellen, Gene Kelly | "New York, New York": Frank Sinatra, Jules Munshin, Gene Kelly

Sinatra sailor movie, *Anchors Aweigh* (1945). Although a massive hit that nabbed Kelly an Oscar nomination, it was conventional and studio-bound, its only innovation being Kelly's famous cartoon dance with Jerry the Mouse. *On the Town*, by contrast, starts hot and keeps going. Few previous musical sequences matched the open-air exuberance of "New York, New York," with its rapid pace and quick cutting and constant forward momentum, and Kelly's "A Day in New York" ballet with Vera-Ellen sums up a romance as astutely as the "Alter Ego" number in *Cover Girl* had depicted Kelly's conflicted thoughts. In a lesser film, the pairing-off scenes with Munshin, Miller, Sinatra, and Garrett would seem merely ordinary. Here, there's that propulsive energy once again: these sailors have only twenty-four hours, and we feel their urgency to do as much as they can in as little time as possible. It also helps that the cast is so likable, even with Sinatra (still in the early phase of his movie career) as a wallflower instead of a swinger. And thank heaven for Alice Pearce, as hysterically funny here as she would be in later years on TV's *Bewitched*, and even oddly touching.

Far from being representative of the original play, *On the Town* is virtually a new work, or at least a reimagined one. It's also, with its imagination and endless high spirits, a genuine delight.

"A Day in New York" ballet: Gene Kelly and Vera-Ellen in a scene cut from the final version

WHAT'S MORE

Although his career was in decline by 1949, Frank Sinatra still had quite a large, and sometimes vociferous, fan base. Fearing possible riots, MGM did its best to keep secret the fact that he would be doing a short scene in Little Italy, but word leaked out anyway. It was all the NYPD could do to keep thousands of devotees at bay long enough for Sinatra to do his scene, then run to a patrol car and speed away.

• • •

The gigantic *Tyrannosaurus rex* in the "Prehistoric Man" number was an entirely made-at-Metro creation, fabricated out of corrugated paper and meticulously wired so that it could be reassembled, after its climactic collapse, to permit retakes. As it worked out, the first take was the charm, and Rex did not need to be put together again.

MUSICALLY SPEAKING

"New York, New York," the best-known song from both the show and the film, required toning down for the big screen. Instead of "a helluva town," it became merely a "wonderful" one. (Perhaps coincidentally, *Wonderful Town* became the title of the next hit show written by Bernstein, Comden, and Green.) The censors also had a problem, in "Prehistoric Man," with the word "libido." While Ann Miller was not permitted to say or sing the word, the argument could certainly be made that she was able to dance about it!

MORE TO SEE

Best Foot Forward (1943): Lucille Ball in a more faithful Technicolor Broadway transfer

Summer Stock (1950): Kelly and Judy Garland, harmoniously paired for a final time

"You Can Count on Me": Alice Pearce, Frank Sinatra, Betty Garrett, Gene Kelly, Ann Miller, Jules Munshin

ANNIE GET YOUR GUN

MGM, 1950 | **COLOR** (TECHNICOLOR), **107 MINUTES**

DIRECTOR: **GEORGE SIDNEY**   PRODUCER: **ARTHUR FREED**   SCREENPLAY: **SIDNEY SHELDON, BASED ON THE MUSICAL PLAY BY HERBERT FIELDS AND DOROTHY FIELDS**   SONGS: **IRVING BERLIN**   CHOREOGRAPHER: **ROBERT ALTON**   STARRING: **BETTY HUTTON (ANNIE OAKLEY), HOWARD KEEL (FRANK BUTLER), LOUIS CALHERN (COLONEL BUFFALO BILL CODY), J. CARROLL NAISH (CHIEF SITTING BULL), EDWARD ARNOLD (PAWNEE BILL), KEENAN WYNN (CHARLIE DAVENPORT), BENAY VENUTA (DOLLY TATE), CLINTON SUNDBERG (FOSTER WILSON), BRAD MORROW (LITTLE JAKE OAKLEY)**

A backwoods sharpshooter finds fame, love, and rivalry when she joins a Wild West show.

It was a big show and became an even bigger film, one that turned out pretty swell despite a great deal of production trouble. With Ethel Merman and a rich Irving Berlin score, *Annie Get Your Gun* had been a major hit on the stage. To acquire the property, MGM paid a greater sum ($650,000) than had yet been spent for the right to film a musical show. The role of Annie Oakley was earmarked for MGM's own musical superstar, Judy Garland, and opposite her was a leading man new to film, baritone Howard Keel. The choice of Busby Berkeley as director struck some as odd; his recent work had been uneven and he had clashed with Garland on previous films. Soon enough, Garland's health problems led to delays and absences, while Berkeley yelled repeatedly at the crew and showed no affinity for the material. Even Keel posed a problem when he fell off a horse and broke his ankle. Finally, Arthur Freed fired Berkeley and MGM suspended Garland, after which her doctor had her hospitalized. Then a final blow: the death of Frank Morgan, originally cast as Buffalo Bill. To replace Garland, the studio borrowed Betty Hutton from Paramount. Some questioned this choice, and the enormous total expense, yet most were pleased at the end result. Perhaps Irving Berlin was an exception, since it was evidently at his behest that *Annie* was withdrawn in 1973 and kept out of circulation. For many years, it was completely unavailable for viewing or broadcast, a situation that finally changed some years after Berlin's death.

It's plain from the get-go that this big and bright production is, unlike many predecessors, quite faithful to its Broadway source. Indeed, director Sidney sometimes opts for too stagy an atmosphere, while other scenes, such as the Wild West show and the skeet-shooting episode, benefit immensely from the fresh-air approach. As for Betty Hutton: seldom will anyone, anywhere, see a performer work so hard. Her rendition of "You Can't Get a Man with a Gun" can serve as a test case for viewers, since few major performances in all musical cinema are so dependent on an individual's taste. Some find her Annie frenetic and even exhausting, while others feel it works just fine. (A few go so far as to take both positions.) Unquestionably, she's deep into the role, and her reprise of "There's No Business Like Show Business" is genuinely affecting. She starts quietly and then builds steadily as

she looks straight out at the audience the whole time. It's both theatrical and cinematic, like the entire film, and devastatingly sincere. Where Howard Keel is concerned, there's less room for dispute: he sings superbly, looks the part, and gives the role exactly what it needs.

A high-powered package of color and entertainment, *Annie Get Your Gun* helped to divert musical filmmaking from its older paths toward the more overtly Broadway-derived movie style to come. With its fine songs, bountiful production, and valiant star, it's a striking demonstration of the craft and resources of the big-studio system. No, they don't make them like this anymore.

Betty Hutton and director George Sidney on the set

WHAT'S MORE

It was clear here, as it has been in subsequent stage productions, that Annie Oakley is a difficult role to cast. Judy Garland may or may not have been suited to it, and after she left the production it was not easy to find a suitable replacement. Twentieth Century-Fox refused to loan out Betty Grable, Betty Garrett's agent asked for too much money, and Ginger Rogers was judged too refined. (Rogers was so desperate for the role that she offered to do it for one dollar.) Another candidate was Judy Canova, who could have sung the dickens out of it. Ditto newcomer Doris Day, who got a shot at an Annie-like role—Calamity Jane—three years later. As for Ethel Merman, it seems that, as usual, she was not a serious contender for the film version, a situation that drew no comment from her and, doubtless, no joy.

• • •

If *Annie* stayed a good deal closer to the original than most film adaptations, it still partook of the practice of dropping songs. Besides leaving out a trivial young-love subplot with two songs, MGM also cut "I'm a Bad, Bad Man," "Moonshine Lullaby," and the gorgeous "I Got Lost in His Arms." Irving Berlin did write one new song for the film, a so-so ballad called "Let's Go West Again." Garland recorded it and Hutton filmed it, after which it ended up going the way of the show's other deleted songs.

Top "Doin' What Comes Naturally": Betty Hutton, Brad Morrow, Diane Dick, Susan Odin, Eleanor Brown | **Bottom** "There's No Business Like Show Business": Betty Hutton

ANNIE GET YOUR GUN

"You Can't Get a Man with a Gun": Betty Hutton

MUSICALLY SPEAKING

"I'm an Indian Too" is one of only two numbers Garland filmed, and makes for fascinating comparisons with the number as it was reshot. Aside from not being in her best voice when she recorded it, Garland appears ill at ease in the footage. Hutton has no such problems, and it was wise of choreographer Alton to rework the staging to remove that spectral white-painted warrior who made Garland's version all the more unsettling. No prizes, at any rate, for figuring out why the song is now regularly dropped from stage productions. As has already been noted: musicals may be forever, but times change.

MORE TO SEE

Call Me Madam (1953): Ethel Merman in a Berlin hit

Kiss Me Kate (1953): Howard Keel in another Broadway smash–turned–musical

Louis Calhern, Howard Keel, Betty Hutton, Keenan Wynn

AN AMERICAN IN PARIS

MGM, 1951 | COLOR (TECHNICOLOR), 113 MINUTES

DIRECTOR: VINCENTE MINNELLI   PRODUCER: ARTHUR FREED   SCREENPLAY: ALAN JAY LERNER   CHOREOGRAPHER: GENE KELLY
SONGS: GEORGE GERSHWIN (MUSIC) AND IRA GERSHWIN (LYRICS)   STARRING: GENE KELLY (JERRY MULLIGAN), LESLIE CARON
(LISE BOUVIER), OSCAR LEVANT (ADAM COOK), GEORGES GUÉTARY (HENRI BAUREL), NINA FOCH (MILO ROBERTS), MADGE BLAKE
(EDNA MAE BESTRAM), HAYDEN RORKE (TOMMY BALDWIN), NOEL NEILL (AMERICAN GIRL)

An expatriate painter is pursued by an American heiress while he romances a young Parisian.

In many minds, *An American in Paris* is the quintessential MGM musical and, with its history-making ballet, a momentous achievement by any standard.

Some movies, it seems, are inevitable. This one came together because several talented people possessed, and shared, overlapping ideas. Gene Kelly wanted to do a story about an ex-G.I. in postwar Paris; Arthur Freed wanted to buy the rights to the George Gershwin tone poem *An American in Paris*; Ira Gershwin wanted a film that featured songs he wrote with his brother. By the time all these intersected, the concept had expanded to include director Minnelli and writer Lerner.

As with *On the Town*, some initial thought of location filming was quickly extinguished

due to cost and difficulty. Fortunately, some authentically French compensation arrived with the casting of a teenaged ballerina, Leslie Caron, whom Kelly had spotted dancing in Paris. For both Kelly and Minnelli, everything in the production revolved around its title ballet. With decor based on the works of Dufy, Renoir, Utrillo, Rousseau, Van Gogh, and Toulouse-Lautrec, it was conceived as an answer to the superb sequence in the British film *The Red Shoes* (1948). Although Kelly had already pushed dance into new realms in *Cover Girl*, *The Pirate* (1948), and *On the Town*, this would be the most ambitious number of its kind yet seen in an American film. It was, as it turned out, a knockout, as was Caron. With the Best Picture and six more Oscars, plus a huge return on MGM's investment, it succeeded on all counts.

An American in Paris was and is an unquestioned triumph, yet perhaps its greatness takes a while to manifest itself. For some, MGM's "Made in Hollywood USA" does not always seem the most convincing substitute for the real City of Light, and Oscar Levant's dream sequence (performing Gershwin's Concerto in F) may feel overlong. Fortunately, Levant also has some genuinely amusing wisecracks, Kelly has never been more brashly charismatic, and Nina Foch makes her acquisitive rich girl unusually compelling. Caron, for her part, is

"American in Paris" ballet: Gene Kelly

adorable, and clearly she was unlike anyone ever before seen in American film. Her superbly imaginative introductory scene is a key to much of the film's success.

Minnelli and Kelly, when given the opportunity, work at a level of confidence and artistry extremely rare in musicals. The utmost manifestation of those gifts comes, naturally, in that final ballet, and don't even consider watching it on a small screen. The detail, color, movement, and sound are all but overwhelming, proving that sometimes a film should be structured to save its greatest assets for nearly the end. In the last Best Picture–winning musical prior to this, *The Great Ziegfeld*, the "money number" ("A Pretty Girl Is Like a Melody") came midway through, making the second half an anticlimax. No such problem here—there's the ballet, a brief post-coda, and the end title. Then we exit, stunned and thrilled.

For Kelly and Minnelli, *An American in Paris* was both affirmation and summit, to be followed by further victories and even more triumph. They would never, however, match that ballet. And, since some great achievements can't be equaled, neither would anyone else.

"I'll Build a Stairway to Paradise": Georges Guétary

WHAT'S MORE

After Maurice Chevalier's wartime activities were judged to be questionable, the role of Henri Baurel, Lise's fiancé, went to Georges Guétary. A quintessentially French entertainer, Guétary had in reality been born in Egypt to Greek parents, and "I'll Build a Stairway to Paradise" was the only solo of the three he originally shot to make the final cut. Getting the stairs to illuminate at the touch of Guétary's foot took some doing, and the oppressively hot Technicolor lights were hard on those showgirls who were frozen in place, but it was all worth the trouble.

• • •

It used to be that a Broadway show would eventually be made into a movie, not the other way around. By the twenty-first century, that once-standard equation was being reversed, and the 2015 Broadway production of *An American in Paris* was decidedly among the most acclaimed of these Hollywood-to-Broadway adaptations. Many had wondered if it could possibly work onstage, and cheering audiences and multiple awards seemed to indicate that yes, indeed, it could.

Top to Bottom | Leslie Caron and Gene Kelly | Leslie Caron | "I Got Rhythm": Gene Kelly

MUSICALLY SPEAKING

Given that the ballet was always intended as the cornerstone of *An American in Paris*, it's remarkable that, except for Gershwin's score, it was not conceived or planned until essentially everything else had been filmed. After the main production stopped, Minnelli went off and shot an entire film (*Father's Little Dividend*) while Kelly worked with the dancers. Then they reunited to shoot the ballet and, lastly, the brief final scene. If such methods seem a little haphazard for the MGM "Dream Factory," in this case they ended up working out just fine.

MORE TO SEE

The Red Shoes (1948): Far more drama than musical, with that legendary title ballet

Lili (1953): Again, not a traditional musical and, with Leslie Caron, enchanting

Above Nina Foch and Gene Kelly | **Below** "American in Paris" ballet: Gene Kelly and Leslie Caron

SINGIN' IN THE RAIN

MGM, 1952 | COLOR (TECHNICOLOR), 103 MINUTES

DIRECTORS AND CHOREOGRAPHERS: STANLEY DONEN AND GENE KELLY   PRODUCER: ARTHUR FREED   SCREENPLAY: BETTY COMDEN AND ADOLPH GREEN   SONGS: NACIO HERB BROWN (MUSIC) AND ARTHUR FREED (LYRICS)   STARRING: GENE KELLY (DON LOCKWOOD), DONALD O'CONNOR (COSMO BROWN), DEBBIE REYNOLDS (KATHY SELDEN), JEAN HAGEN (LINA LAMONT), MILLARD MITCHELL (R. F. SIMPSON), CYD CHARISSE (DANCER), DOUGLAS FOWLEY (ROSCOE DEXTER), RITA MORENO (ZELDA ZANDERS), KATHLEEN FREEMAN (PHOEBE DINSMORE), MADGE BLAKE (DORA BAILEY)

The advent of talking pictures affects the careers of a romantic star and his leading lady.

Many feel that it's the best of the best, and the most entertaining movie musical ever made. How and why, exactly, did it get to this summit? Some answers are obvious, and a few aren't. One thing is certain: they weren't reaching for greatness.

In 1950, Arthur Freed assigned Betty Comden and Adolph Green to write a script around the songs he had written with Nacio Herb Brown in the late 1920s and early 1930s. Amiable as it was, the Brown/Freed catalog was hardly on a Gershwin level, so there was little thought about artistry. As they worked, Comden and Green moved from writing a script *of* the era in which the songs were written to one *about* it:

the moment when silent films ended and talkies and musicals began. Although the script simplified the actual chronology of the changeover to sound, many details were essentially accurate, and as it all began to come together, the currents of history seemed to guide the production to take on something of a life of its own. MGM veterans, recalling the most chaotic time in their professional lives, began to ransack their memories and studio warehouses for recollections and mementos.

Gene Kelly, just finishing *An American in Paris*, would star and co-direct with Stanley Donen, and as before there would be a teenage leading lady without extensive film experience. In this case it was Debbie Reynolds, being faced with her first major professional challenge; pushed hard by Kelly and Donen, she strove mightily and successfully to keep up with the expert talent around her. Donald O'Connor, compelled to offer a tribute to comedy, surpassed himself with "Make 'em Laugh," while Jean Hagen, brilliantly cast as a movie queen with a voice of brass and a heart of granite, gave a knockout comedy performance. (She was also versatile: that's her, not Reynolds, doing the dubbing when Lina is given a cultured speaking voice.) And Kelly did his finest on-screen work, wryly sending up his own image and getting through the torrential shoot of that legendary title number in a mere day and a half.

Everyone at MGM was happy with the result, and both the reviews and receipts were favorable, if less enthusiastic than those of *An American in Paris*. Then, as time passed and perspective shifted, something began to be much

Top "You Were Meant for Me": Debbie Reynolds and Gene Kelly
Bottom "Moses Supposes": Donald O'Connor and Gene Kelly

clearer than it had been in 1952: this movie had just about every good and grand thing that a musical could deliver and none of the downsides. Plus, wonder of Comden-Green wonders, the script was as good as the musical numbers. And those numbers! From lyrical to boisterous, each is a gem. "Make 'em Laugh" was epic, "Good Morning" a true rouser, and the title song simply perfect. No, the big "Broadway Rhythm Ballet" could never have happened in a real 1929 musical, but, as danced by Kelly and Charisse, it's as fabulous, as essential, as everything else.

One of the true marvels of *Singin' in the Rain* is how, even after dozens of viewings, its magic does not diminish. Without intending to, and without overreaching, Kelly, Donen, Freed, and everyone else masterfully demonstrated just how good a musical could be. By returning to the genre's very beginnings, they created a work that spans the entirety of musicals, past to future, in a way that is utterly timeless and completely joyous.

Producer/lyricist Arthur Freed and Jean Hagen on the set

Left Gene Kelly | **Above** Douglas Fowley, Gene Kelly, Jean Hagen, Kathleen Freeman

WHAT'S MORE

Real-life parallels, somewhat exaggerated for effect, were definitely part of the mix here. Lina Lamont was primarily a composite of silent diva Mae Murray and Billie Dawn in *Born Yesterday*, a role created by Comden and Green's good friend Judy Holliday. There were also actors in the early sound era who, like Ms. Lamont, required dubbing by others. These include, in 1929, the heavily accented Anny Ondra in Alfred Hitchcock's *Blackmail* and Paul Lukas in *The* [first!] *Wolf of Wall Street*. There was even a kind of cinematic forerunner: a 1946 French production, *Étoile sans lumière* (*Star without Light*), starring Édith Piaf as a nobody who supplies the voice for a vain silent film queen. The tone is different, yet similarities are very present.

• • •

Strange but disappointingly true: Gene Kelly never again starred in (or directed) a commercially successful movie musical after this. Good, yes—profitable, no. (*That's Entertainment!*, being a documentary, is a special exception.) For Debbie Reynolds, there would be many more hits, including one musical (*The Unsinkable Molly Brown*). She famously said that *Singin' in the Rain* and childbirth were the toughest things she ever did, and when she died in 2016, it was no surprise that nearly every obituary recalled the breakthrough performance in the film she herself considered the greatest one she would ever make.

MUSICALLY SPEAKING

As with *An American in Paris*, the big ballet near the end was not conceived or budgeted until after production had begun, and at $600,000, it cost even more than its predecessor. It was not, however, intended as a climax to the action, as the earlier one had been. There is even an in-joke to that effect when, after the entire thing unfolds on the screen, the studio head comments, "I can't quite visualize it." As for Cyd Charisse in the ballet, neither the studio head nor anybody else could possibly have visualized anything, or anyone, this spectacular.

> ### MORE TO SEE
>
> *Sally* (1929): Broadway diva Marilyn Miller in her defining role
>
> *It's Always Fair Weather* (1955): Another witty Comden/Green script, directed by Kelly and Donen

"Good Morning": Donald O'Connor, Debbie Reynolds, Gene Kelly

"Singin' in the Rain": Gene Kelly

MILLION DOLLAR MERMAID

MGM, 1952 | COLOR (TECHNICOLOR), 115 MINUTES

DIRECTOR: MERVYN LEROY   PRODUCER: ARTHUR HORNBLOW JR.   SCREENPLAY: EVERETT FREEMAN   WATER BALLET DIRECTOR: BUSBY BERKELEY   STARRING: ESTHER WILLIAMS (ANNETTE KELLERMAN), VICTOR MATURE (JAMES SULLIVAN), WALTER PIDGEON (FREDERICK KELLERMAN), DAVID BRIAN (ALFRED HARPER), DONNA CORCORAN (ANNETTE, AGE TEN), JESSE WHITE (DOC CRONNOL), MARIA TALLCHIEF (ANNA PAVLOVA), HOWARD FREEMAN (ALDRICH), CHARLES WATTS (POLICEMAN)

Annette Kellerman leaves Australia and finds fame as a swimmer, movie star, and advocate for the one-piece bathing suit.

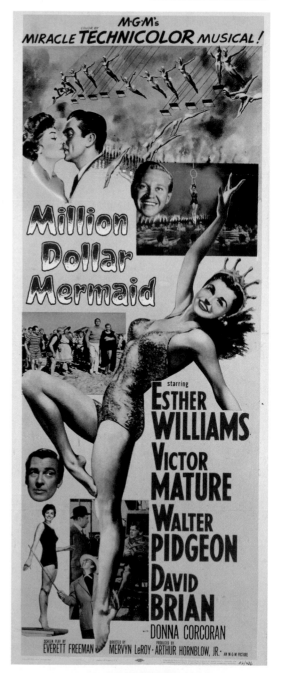

Esther Williams swam, and the whole world watched. One of MGM's elites for over a decade, she carved, or dived, out a niche that no one else has ever filled. Although only tangentially a musical, *Million Dollar Mermaid* is the movie that best explains to the world what she was all about.

Back in big-studio days, a musical didn't necessarily depend on the greatest talents in song and dance. Voice and dance doubles were always ready to help, and a few performers thrived by having completely different skills. So it was with Ms. Williams, a champion swimmer who, without a great deal of fuss, ended up a major-league star. While the template for her career was that of Olympic skater Sonja Henie, Williams outdid the model by faring quite well, too, on dry land. She was pretty, could sing pleasantly and move attractively, and her scripts played to her assets by nearly always keeping things light and amusing. From *Bathing Beauty*, in 1944, onward, her films were monster hits, the kind of enterprises that easily absorbed the losses from some of MGM's dicier ventures. Even her less inspired films, such as *Fiesta*, filled the studio coffers when other movies tanked, and the better Williams pictures were, and remain, genuinely entertaining. *Neptune's Daughter* featured the classic song "Baby, It's Cold Outside," while *Take Me Out to the Ball Game* found her keeping up nicely with Gene Kelly and Frank Sinatra. There's much amusement, too, in such bonbons as *On an Island with You*, *Easy to Love*, and the inevitably titled *Dangerous When Wet*.

Although *Million Dollar Mermaid* was advertised as "MGM's Miracle Technicolor Musical!" it should, more properly, be termed a lightly embellished biopic with a brief ballet (by the gorgeous Maria Tallchief) and two epic water spectacles. Early in the twentieth century, Annette Kellerman gained fame as a champion

Esther Williams and her supporting cast

swimmer, vaudeville star, and crusader for comfortable bathing suits for women. A little later, she was the first swimming movie star, and who besides Esther Williams could possibly play her? Since Kellerman did her act in a glass tank at New York's mammoth Hippodrome Theater, MGM did the Hollywood thing and engaged Busby Berkeley, who was as suited to spectacular staging as Williams was to play Kellerman. The resulting two sequences—one with colored smoke and trapezes, the other involving spraying water—were the most dazzling of Williams's career. A generation later, when excerpted for MGM's valedictory movie-musical salute, *That's Entertainment!*, the Berkeley numbers stopped the show cold. Audiences who had not thought about Williams in years (she was retired by then) were entranced by her graceful physicality, Berkeley's spectacle, and the sheer audacity of it all, which somehow transcended camp. It goes without saying that while the remainder of *Million Dollar Mermaid* is not quite as invigorating as these two scenes, its good-natured and sometimes poignant recounting of a fascinating career fits its star as well as any of her swimsuits.

One doesn't go to Esther Williams films for greatness or profundity, but take them, and Ms. Williams, for what they are, and that will be plenty. She played a million dollar mermaid because she actually *was* one and, wet or dry, little else matters.

Top to Bottom | Victor Mature and Esther Williams | Maria Tallchief and Esther Williams | Esther Williams, Walter Pidgeon, Wilton Graff, Jesse White, Victor Mature, Charles Watts

1567-93

Esther Williams

WHAT'S MORE

The two things most viewers recall about *Million Dollar Mermaid*, apart from the Berkeley spectacles, are Kellerman's arrest for wearing a one-piece swimsuit, and her glass tank shattering while she shoots one of her movies. Both incidents were factual, even if MGM intensified their drama a bit. The arrest was in 1907, in Massachusetts, and the tank mishap occurred in 1914 while Kellerman was filming *Neptune's Daughter* (not the Esther Williams version). Though she received lacerations, she was not as badly hurt as the film's director, Herbert Brenon, who was in the tank with her.

• • •

Ms. Williams did not need to search far for a title for her 1999 autobiography: [*The*] *Million Dollar Mermaid* easily took care of that. A few revelations in the book were quite sensational, and some suspicions were validated when she later admitted that she had "heightened" a few details to boost sales. One tidbit that probably did not require augmenting was her account of a steamy affair with her *Mermaid* costar, Victor Mature. Their onscreen chemistry is quite evident, so it's no surprise that little acting was involved.

MUSICALLY SPEAKING

The first of the two Busby Berkeley spectacles features Williams in a gold mesh body suit, wearing a small crown on her head. Pay special attention to the crown, which was made of inflexible aluminum. When she executed the fifty-foot dive off the pedestal, Williams landed hard on that crown, which caused her to break three vertebrae in her neck and spend months in a body cast. It was much later, in a wry tone, that Williams recalled of the demanding and sometimes erratic Berkeley that "Busby didn't care whether you got killed or not." For this hard-driving director, such sacrifices simply went with the territory.

MORE TO SEE

Neptune's Daughter (1949): Williams as, what else, a bathing suit designer

Easy to Love (1953): Another hazardous Williams/Berkeley spectacle, on water skis. And she was pregnant!

Esther Williams and Charles Watts

GENTLEMEN PREFER BLONDES

TWENTIETH CENTURY-FOX, 1953 | COLOR (TECHNICOLOR), 91 MINUTES

DIRECTOR: HOWARD HAWKS   PRODUCER: SOL C. SIEGEL   SCREENPLAY: CHARLES LEDERER, BASED ON THE MUSICAL PLAY BY JOSEPH FIELDS, FROM THE NOVEL BY ANITA LOOS   SONGS: JULE STYNE (MUSIC) AND LEO ROBIN (LYRICS), HOAGY CARMICHAEL (MUSIC) AND HAROLD ADAMSON (LYRICS)   CHOREOGRAPHER: JACK COLE   STARRING: JANE RUSSELL (DOROTHY SHAW), MARILYN MONROE (LORELEI LEE), CHARLES COBURN (SIR FRANCIS BEEKMAN), ELLIOTT REID (ERNIE MALONE), TOMMY NOONAN (GUS ESMOND JR.), GEORGE WINSLOW (HENRY SPOFFORD III), MARCEL DALIO (MAGISTRATE), TAYLOR HOLMES (MR. ESMOND SR.), NORMA VARDEN (LADY BEEKMAN), GEORGE CHAKIRIS (DANCER [UNCREDITED])

Two entertainers go to Paris. One is a blonde who loves diamonds, the other a brunette who likes men.

A classic musical, unquestionably, with a few twists. The standard virtues of song, dance, and eye-catching production are all present, yet the most powerful charge comes from the iconography. Marilyn Monroe is at her most incandescent, and Jane Russell is pretty sensational, too.

Anita Loos's tale of the winsome gold-digger Lorelei Lee had pretty much defined the Jazz Age, and the Broadway show made a star of Carol Channing. For the movies, the 1920s setting would be jettisoned along with most of the plot and songs. Normally, such alterations are the main reason some people loathe the

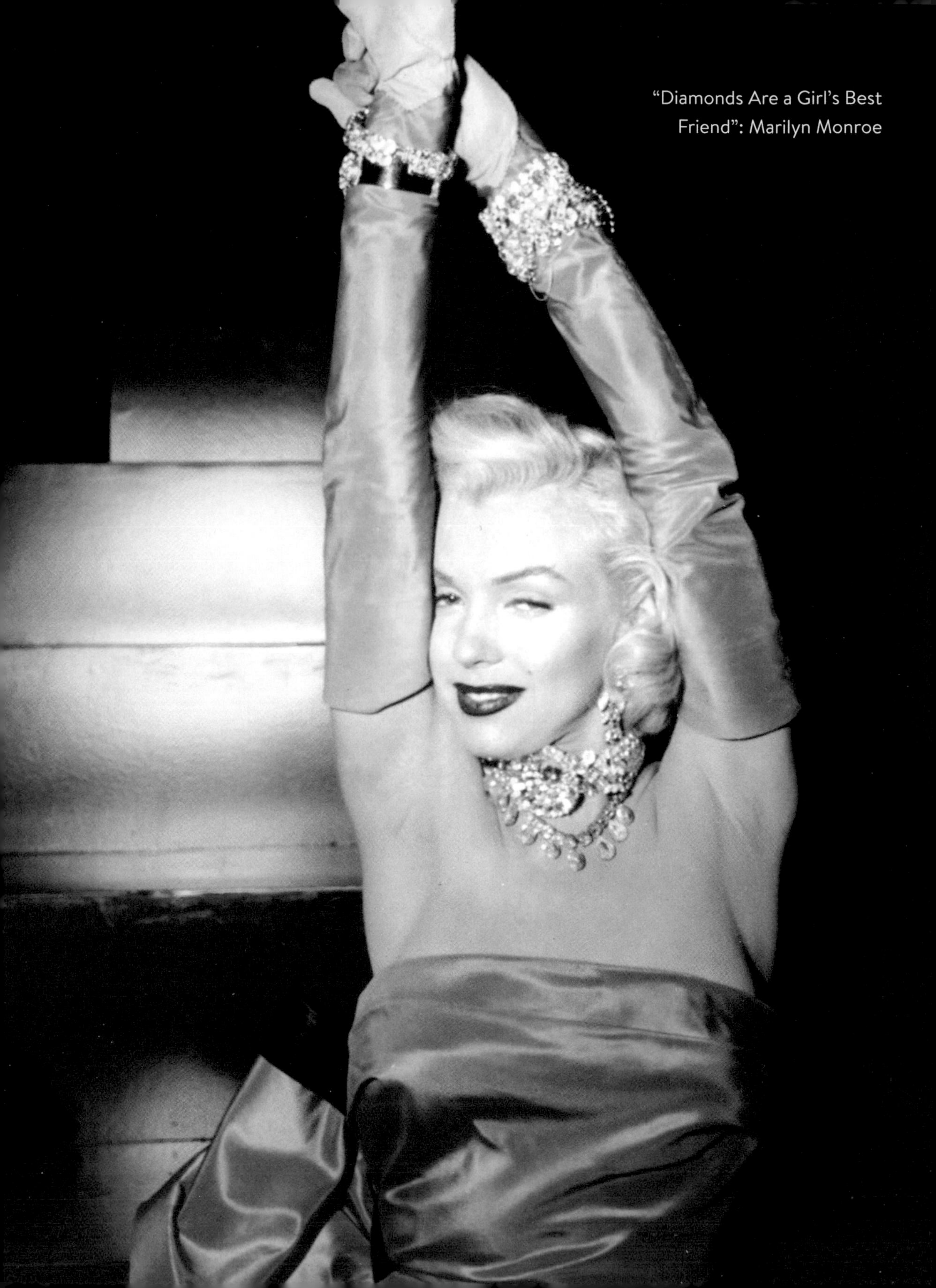

"Diamonds Are a Girl's Best Friend": Marilyn Monroe

notion of a movie version of a hit show. Here, somehow, the changes are not so much distorting or reductive as they are transformational. With a great comedy director in Hawks, and a fine choreographer, Jack Cole, *Gentlemen Prefer Blondes* becomes its own entity. It is, in a way, one of the first "reimagined" musical adaptations, like *Cabaret* (1972) or *Chicago* (2002). Essentially, it's a movie about friendship, with Monroe and Russell as the kind of pals whose bond can withstand and endure anything, up to and including jail, blackmail, and an Olympic team. Apart from similar career choices and figures, they have little in common, yet always maintain their mutual devotion and respect. Dorothy has seen it all, Lorelei is a master of faux-innocent manipulation, and in tandem they form one of the great teams in all film.

Russell was the bigger star when this film was made, being paid far more money and receiving top billing. For Monroe, just coming into her own, there had been some initial thought that (a) she wasn't up to the musical sequences and (b) Fox's game, if fading, musical queen, Betty Grable, should be Lorelei. (Channing was never seriously considered for the role.) Where Russell had little to prove, Monroe had everything, and in the end, demonstrated her talent as both a comic actor and a musical performer. It's unfortunate that her two later musicals (*There's No Business Like Show Business* and *Let's Make Love*) allowed her fewer opportunities than she had here, let alone a song as definitive as "Diamonds Are a Girl's Best Friend." For Russell, an extremely likable performer and an excellent singer, this would be a career highlight. The pity is that her career was governed by the coarse tastes of her discoverer, Howard Hughes.

"Ain't There Anyone Here for Love?": Jane Russell

Both Monroe and Russell responded especially well to the demanding Jack Cole, who had a special knack for displaying women of middling dance ability to their best advantage. Monroe and Russell strut and amble and gesture, and between their personalities and Cole's staging, the musical sequences come together just fine. Under the sharp guidance of director Hawks, they do just as well in the comedy scenes, which truly is saying something.

Many later viewers came to *Gentlemen Prefer Blondes* through Madonna's "Material Girl" music video, in which the look and staging of the "Diamonds" number are copied relentlessly. It was typically audacious and smart of Madonna to hitch her wagon to Monroe's star, and what's also clear is that the original remains untouchable. It may have started out as a shiny pop entertainment, but life and stardom are both funny things, and *Gentlemen Prefer Blondes* ended up as a milestone.

WHAT'S MORE

Anita Loos did not contribute to the script of either this film or the Broadway show, and some predicted that the many changes to her story would leave her aghast. For a while, expecting the worst, she put off seeing the movie. When she finally capitulated and watched it, she was delighted. Her Lorelei, she decided, was a good enough character to withstand all manner of alteration, and she found Monroe perfectly dandy.

• • •

As with many other films, more musical sequences were shot than actually used. The biggest one was a Parisian number featuring Monroe, Russell, and Gwen Verdon, who also helped Jack Cole with the choreography. A tiny piece of it can be seen in the original *Blondes* coming-attractions trailer. In one number that *did* make it in, a "mistake" was allowed to remain. At the end of Cole's hilariously homoerotic "Ain't There Anyone Here for Love?," Russell was not originally supposed to fall into the pool—but it was such a funny touch that everyone agreed to keep it.

Marilyn Monroe, Elliott Reid, Jane Russell

MUSICALLY SPEAKING

The "Diamonds Are a Girl's Best Friend" now seen in the film was not the one Cole originally envisioned. He had planned to have Monroe in a faux eighteenth-century setting, wearing little more than a gem-encrusted bikini. Since she was already a flash point for touchy censors, Cole was ordered to reconceive the number with a raft of chorus boys and a less-exposed, tightly corseted star. The rest, as they say, is history.

MORE TO SEE

On the Riviera (1951): Cole choreography and Danny Kaye

Les Girls (1957): Two Coles—Jack and Porter— plus Gene Kelly

Top "A Little Girl from Little Rock": Marilyn Monroe and Jane Russell
Bottom Elliott Reid, Jane Russell, Marilyn Monroe, Tommy Noonan

THE BAND WAGON

MGM, 1953 | **COLOR** (TECHNICOLOR), **112 MINUTES**

DIRECTOR: **VINCENTE MINNELLI**   PRODUCER: **ARTHUR FREED**   SCREENPLAY: **BETTY COMDEN AND ADOLPH GREEN**   SONGS: **ARTHUR SCHWARTZ (MUSIC) AND HOWARD DIETZ (LYRICS)**   CHOREOGRAPHER: **MICHAEL KIDD**   STARRING: **FRED ASTAIRE** (TONY HUNTER), **CYD CHARISSE** (GABRIELLE GERARD), **OSCAR LEVANT** (LESTER MARTON), **NANETTE FABRAY** (LILY MARTON), **JACK BUCHANAN** (JEFFREY CORDOVA), **JAMES MITCHELL** (PAUL BYRD), **ROBERT GIST** (HAL), **LEROY DANIELS** (ARCADE SHOESHINE MAN), **AVA GARDNER** (HERSELF)

A has-been movie star and a ballerina clash with each other and their director when they are teamed in a new Broadway musical.

Fred Astaire occupied the center of the movie musical universe for four decades, and in many ways still does. *The Band Wagon*, one of his supreme achievements, is something of an autobiography for him, and also for Vincente Minnelli and for Comden and Green. From start to finish, it's an authentic delight.

The film sums up the world of theater in as blissful a fashion as *Singin' in the Rain* did with film. Once again, Arthur Freed was determined to celebrate a songwriting team, in this case the lesser-known (if equally accomplished) pairing of composer Arthur Schwartz and Howard Dietz, a talented lyricist who also headed the MGM publicity department. Comden and Green found it difficult to frame these songs until they arrived, in a way, at a mirror. Their plot would detail the creation of a show written by a Comden/Green-like team, starring a former movie star very similar to Astaire, with a director-costar who has a few traits in common with Minnelli. From out-of-town fiasco to Broadway smash, *The Band Wagon*—that's the name of the show, too—covers all the bases. There are creative differences, a fierce clash between a ballerina (Charisse) and a hoofer (Astaire), a pretentious director who needs to be humbled (Buchanan), and battling husband-and-wife writers (Fabray and Levant as Comden and Green, who were not married to each other despite what everybody thought). After the show is pulled together, a splendid series of musical numbers climaxes with Michael Kidd's dazzling "Girl Hunt" ballet. A witty parody of hard-boiled detective fiction à la Mickey Spillane, "Girl Hunt" completes the remarkable dance trilogy that MGM began with the "American in Paris" ballet. Charisse, in both blonde and brunette incarnations, is as sensational as she was in *Singin' in the Rain*, and by straying wildly from type as a tough private eye, Astaire shows the immense breadth of his talent.

At first glance, some of *The Band Wagon* might seem a little calculated and pat, with its "art versus pop" argument and romanticized notion that a show can be so brilliantly improved after starting out as an unadulterated disaster. (Such things used to happen in pre-Broadway

"That's Entertainment": Nanette Fabray, Fred Astaire, Jack Buchanan

tryouts, but to *this* extreme?) Still, with its witty dialogue and loving details, this is a prime example of a musical that gets better with every viewing. One superb song follows another in breathtaking succession: "A Shine on Your Shoes," the swooningly romantic "Dancing in the Dark," the rousing "I Love Louisa," the hilarious/creepy "Triplets." Just as good is the new song Schwarz and Dietz wrote for the film, the grand show-biz anthem "That's Entertainment." Everyone gets a chance to shine, and by the end the feeling is one of sheer bliss.

Tony Hunter, Astaire's *Band Wagon* alter ego, goes to Broadway because his movie career has died. Although Astaire never did make such a return, the sad truth is that many of his 1950s films were financially unsuccessful, this one among them. He managed to endure, of course, and so, happily, does *The Band Wagon*. "That's Entertainment," Minnelli and Astaire and company have announced, and any disagreement is simply not an option.

Top to Bottom | "Dancing in the Dark": Cyd Charisse and Fred Astaire | Fred Astaire and Cyd Charisse | Cyd Charisse, Fred Astaire, Jack Buchanan

It usually takes a great deal of work to make a musical appear effortless. In the case of *The Band Wagon*, that also involved a great deal of tension on the set. Astaire was coping with his wife's terminal illness, Buchanan suffered physical pain, and Levant was recovering from a heart attack. Charisse tended to be shy and aloof, while Minnelli stayed, essentially, in his own world. For the outgoing Fabray, this would be "the coldest, unfriendliest, [and] most terrible experience" she ever had. To everyone's credit, none of this ever shows on the screen; if they had issues, they were also pros.

• • •

MGM, like other studios, was always open to the idea of recycling. The theater in which *The Band Wagon* is set turned up later in 1953 in *Torch Song*, starring Joan Crawford as a hard-driving theatrical diva. Her big number, "Two-Faced Woman" was also a *Band Wagon* retread, filmed with Cyd Charisse and then deleted. *Torch Song* used the same pre-recording by the same voice dubber (India Adams), in a vastly different staging. It featured Crawford in dark makeup as a lusty woman of color. Really.

"A Shine on Your Shoes": Leroy Daniels and Fred Astaire

MUSICALLY SPEAKING

When the initial *Band Wagon* show-within-a-show lays a huge egg (literally), everyone can see why: the "You and the Night and the Music" number shown in rehearsal is an unmitigated, smoke-filled catastrophe. It was also something of an inside joke. Years earlier, Minnelli and Astaire had filmed a sequence in *Ziegfeld Follies* so cataclysmic that it could not be used. Charisse was in that one as well, and instead of pyrotechnics, the original number featured Himalayan mountains of soap bubbles. For everyone concerned, the later scene was a droll reminder that some production concepts just won't work.

MORE TO SEE

Easter Parade (1948): Conventional and delightful, with Garland, Astaire, and Ann Miller

Three Little Words (1950): Astaire and Red Skelton as songwriters Bert Kalmar and Harry Ruby

"Triplets": Fred Astaire, Nanette Fabray, Jack Buchanan

CALAMITY JANE

WARNER BROS., 1953 | COLOR (TECHNICOLOR), 101 MINUTES

DIRECTOR: DAVID BUTLER PRODUCER: WILLIAM JACOBS SCREENPLAY: JAMES O'HANLON SONGS: SAMMY FAIN (MUSIC) AND PAUL FRANCIS WEBSTER (LYRICS) CHOREOGRAPHER: JACK DONOHUE STARRING: DORIS DAY (CALAMITY JANE), HOWARD KEEL (WILD BILL HICKOK), ALLYN [ANN] MCLERIE (KATIE BROWN), PHILIP CAREY (LIEUTENANT DANNY GILMARTIN), DICK WESSON (FRANCIS FRYER), PAUL HARVEY (HENRY MILLER), CHUBBY JOHNSON (RATTLESNAKE), GALE ROBBINS (ADELAID ADAMS)

A hot-tempered scout in the Dakota Territory realizes that there's more to life than rifles and buckskins.

Few singers ever hit film with the impact of Doris Day. Although she's remembered more for her later comedies with Rock Hudson and others, most of her first decade in movies was spent in musicals. If some of those were not consistently of the highest quality, *Calamity Jane* is a major exception, and she's terrific in it.

Clearly, there would be no *Calamity Jane* without *Annie Get Your Gun*, which is not a criticism of either film; they even share the same leading man. While not necessarily better than *Annie*—an arguable point—*Calamity* is less beholden to theatrical conventions and has a more cinematic feel. It also has, under veteran director David Butler, a rambunctious enthusiasm that sets it apart from many other musicals

of its time. The screenplay has some enjoyable twists, the pacing is consistently upbeat, and the songs are excellent. Besides the classic, Oscar-winning "Secret Love," the most arresting number is that "Deadwood Stage" piece that opens and closes the movie; once heard, its "Whip crack-a-way" line is permanently embedded in most viewers' minds.

Calamity is, quite simply, one of the best roles Doris Day ever had, and if the character is conceived as a close relative of Annie Oakley, Day makes her seem entirely different. Rarely, in a musical, is anyone, male or female, permitted to be this physical, to which Day responds with a kind of liberated joy that is captivating. Calamity runs and leaps and shoots until she finally is tamed, and Day stays gloriously on-target the whole way. As one of the rare singers who could really act, she clearly understands the links between speech and song, action and reaction, being vocal and being silent. The only pity, in all this, is that she so seldom had the opportunities she seizes here so triumphantly. With musicals in decline, she moved on to the comedies that made her an even bigger star without always making the best use of such a big-league talent. One *Calamity Jane* is worth any number of *Do Not Disturb*s or some of the others, and small

wonder that Day later cited the role of Calamity as her favorite. There is also, here, the strong and sturdy presence (and great voice) of Howard Keel, and Allyn McLerie is as pert and vibrant as she was, the previous year, in Butler's lovely *Where's Charley?*

Ironically, *Calamity Jane* didn't do as well at the box office as a number of less worthy Day films. If this was not her fault, it scarcely offered her much incentive to keep exploring musical territory. All the more reason, then, to treasure her spectacular turn as Calamity Jane: a beloved, abundantly gifted artist is given truly outstanding material, and the result is wonderfully spontaneous musical combustion.

Doris Day and Allyn McLerie

WHAT'S MORE

Calamity Jane is an early example of a practice that would later become excessively prevalent: a movie musical subsequently reconfigured for the stage. It was first done that way in 1961, and Carol Burnett performed the role live and on television. Allyn [Ann] McLerie repeated her film role in one production, while other theater Calamities have included Martha Raye and Ginger Rogers. The show has been frequently performed in the UK and Australia as well as the United States, so evidently *Calamity Jane* can fare quite nicely on its, or her, own.

While it's safe to assume that little of it occurred as a result of conscious subterfuge, *Calamity Jane* has long been seen by some as a carnival of playfully alternative sexuality. There's Calamity herself, who is kidded about her lack of femininity, mistaken for male, and propositioned by a Chicago hooker. There's Francis (Dick Wesson), who goes way over the top in a drag number. There's some rather strong bonding between Calamity and Katie that can be viewed in all sorts of ways. Even Wild Bill Hickok (Keel) is compelled, at one point, to don the attire of a Native American mother. What drew little comment all those years ago sure can set off lots of bells for a modern audience.

"A Woman's Touch": Doris Day and Allyn McLerie

MUSICALLY SPEAKING

If the film itself was a financial disappointment, no one could argue with the success of its hit song. "Secret Love" was near the top of the pop charts for a number of months in 1953–1954, with several weeks in the number one spot. Day, for her part, knew how good it was the first time composer Sammy Fain played it for her. On the day of the recording she rode her bicycle to the studio, went into the booth, and sang it without a rehearsal. After just one take, musical director Ray Heindorf told her, "That's it. You're never going to do it better." She had nailed one of her biggest hits the first time out.

MORE TO SEE

The Harvey Girls (1946): Judy Garland in the Old West

Where's Charley? (1952): Ray Bolger delightfully re-creates his Broadway hit

| **Above** Dick Wesson, Doris Day, Howard Keel, and Allyn McLerie on the set | **Below** Doris Day, Allyn McLerie, Howard Keel |

SEVEN BRIDES
FOR SEVEN BROTHERS

MGM, 1954 | COLOR (ANSCO)/CINEMASCOPE, 102 MINUTES

DIRECTOR: STANLEY DONEN   PRODUCER: JACK CUMMINGS   SCREENPLAY: FRANCES GOODRICH, ALBERT HACKETT, AND DOROTHY KINGSLEY, BASED ON THE STORY "THE SOBBIN' WOMEN" BY STEPHEN VINCENT BENET   SONGS: GENE DE PAUL (MUSIC) AND JOHNNY MERCER (LYRICS)   CHOREOGRAPHER: MICHAEL KIDD   STARRING: HOWARD KEEL (ADAM PONTIPEE), JANE POWELL (MILLY), JACQUES D'AMBOISE (EPHRAIM), MATT MATTOX (CALEB), MARC PLATT (DANIEL), TOMMY RALL (FRANK), JEFF RICHARDS (BENJAMIN), RUSS TAMBLYN (GIDEON), BETTY CARR (SARAH), NORMA DOGGETT (MARTHA), VIRGINIA GIBSON (LIZA), NANCY KILGAS (ALICE), RUTA KILMONIS [LEE] (RUTH), JULIE NEWMEYER [NEWMAR] (DORCAS)

When an Oregon frontiers-man brings home a bride, his six brothers decide to follow suit.

Contrary to legend, this was not a humble "sleeper" that no one cared about until it started to make money. Its great merit was clear from the start even in a time of uncertainty. By 1954, musicals were no longer the guaranteed proposition they had been in the previous decade. Television was a juggernaut, studio production was slowing down, and grosses were shrinking. It was in this shaky climate that *Seven Brides for Seven Brothers* burst through like a shot of adrenaline.

Its roots lay in, of all things, the legendary history of ancient Rome, specifically the abduction of the Sabine women by the male settlers of the newly founded city. The tale was given an Americanized spin by Stephen Vincent Benet in his short story "The Sobbin' Women," set in the Tennessee Valley, and then a team of MGM writers changed the setting to the Oregon Territory in 1850. Director Stanley Donen wanted it shot on location, the studio's money people thought otherwise, and it does look jarring to modern eyes when Jane Powell launches into "Wonderful, Wonderful Day" by moving from an outdoor shot to an extremely artificial soundstage meadow. If filming at the studio was a way of cutting costs this was still, at $2.54 million, one of MGM's biggest productions of the season. (The costliest was *Brigadoon*, which was also denied a location shoot and ended up a major box-office failure.) Cost considerations aside, some were caught off guard at just how massive a sensation *Brides* caused: it became the highest-grossing MGM musical up to that time and was an Academy Award nominee for Best Picture.

The reasons for this popularity and esteem are evident. Thanks to Donen, the pace is almost as sprightly as in *Singin' in the Rain*, and two of MGM's musical stalwarts, Howard Keel and Jane Powell, have never been better. There was also the sense, due to the clever script, that this was racier than most musicals; how many of

Ruta Kilmonis, Matt Mattox, Marc Platt, Norma Doggett, Nancy Kilgas, Russ Tamblyn, Jane Powell, Howard Keel, Betty Carr, Jeff Richards, Tommy Rall, Julie Newmeyer, Virginia Gibson, Jacques D'Amboise

them, after all, end with a shotgun wedding? Most of all, there's the dancing. After a first section devoted to plot and songs, choreographer Michael Kidd takes charge and *Seven Brides* soars. Its centerpiece is the barn raising, where the brothers' budding interest in the local females plays out in a fierce competition with the local swains to see who can build a barn fastest. It isn't simply about dance or athleticism, dazzling as they are. What's most impressive is the storytelling; as with all the great artists creating musicals, Kidd is aware that the sheer display counts for little when not deepening and advancing the plot and characters. He does it again, in a far different key, in "Lonesome Polecat," in which a vivid yet subtle depiction of sexual frustration is clear evidence of how a gifted artist could get "iffy" material past the still-active censors.

Seven Brides was seen as a boisterous and slightly bawdy romp when it was released, in a time when the term "non-consensual" was not part of the language. Not everyone today will be enamored of the sexual politics on display, while others will find it easier to simply shrug, enjoy the show, and accept it as the joyous fable it's intended to be. For those willing to enter into the brightly colored spirit of things, the rewards will include a great deal of entertainment and, most certainly, some of the finest dancing ever put on film.

Top Howard Keel, Jane Powell, and lyricist Johnny Mercer on the set | **Bottom** Jane Powell and Howard Keel

WHAT'S MORE

Michael Kidd insisted that the six dancing Pontipee brothers be drawn from the ranks of the finest talent then available. He got his way for five of them, even if Russ Tamblyn was more a gymnast than a traditional dancer. The sixth brother was MGM contract actor Jeff Richards, an ex-professional baseball player whose dance ability consisted mainly of looking attractive. In most of the dances, he can be seen sitting things out while his brothers cut loose.

• • •

Two of the kidnapped brides may seem familiar to some viewers, and they should. Ruta Kilmonis (Ruth) changed her last name to Lee and became a staple on sitcoms and game shows for several decades. The statuesque Dorcas is Julie Newmeyer, later known as Julie Newmar, who had already appeared in the "Girl Hunt" ballet in *The Band Wagon*. Like Ruta Lee, Ms. Newmar stayed perpetually busy on TV, in film, and on the stage for many years, ever a welcome face (and figure).

Betty Carr, Tommy Rall, Ruta Kilmonis, Matt Mattox, Nancy Kilgas, Russ Tamblyn, Virginia Gibson, Jacques D'Amboise, Norma Doggett, Marc Platt, Julie Newmeyer, Jeff Richards

MUSICALLY SPEAKING

Despite its popularity, this film produced no hit songs. It might have been otherwise had director Donen gone with his original choice of Harold Arlen to compose the music. Unfortunately, lyricist Johnny Mercer thought otherwise and complained to Donen that Arlen was "too picky about the words." The eventual choice was journeyman tunesmith Gene de Paul, who produced quite engaging tunes that were, in the final analysis, not really memorable. As a result, *Seven Brides* is one of the rare big musicals that is truly less about the song and more about the dance.

MORE TO SEE

Deep in My Heart (1954): Donen's biography of composer Sigmund Romberg, with many guest stars

Li'l Abner (1959): The *Seven Brides* songwriters, a Broadway hit, and Julie Newmar as Stupefyin' Jones

A STAR IS BORN

WARNER BROS., 1954 | COLOR (TECHNICOLOR)/CINEMASCOPE, 181 MINUTES (ORIGINAL RUNNING TIME)

DIRECTOR: GEORGE CUKOR   PRODUCER: SIDNEY LUFT   SCREENPLAY: MOSS HART, BASED ON THE SCREENPLAY BY DOROTHY PARKER, ALAN CAMPBELL, AND ROBERT CARSON   SONGS: HAROLD ARLEN (MUSIC) AND IRA GERSHWIN   CHOREOGRAPHER: RICHARD BARSTOW   STARRING: JUDY GARLAND (ESTHER BLODGETT, LATER VICKI LESTER), JAMES MASON (NORMAN MAINE), CHARLES BICKFORD (OLIVER NILES), JACK CARSON (MATT LIBBY), TOM NOONAN (DANNY MCGUIRE), LUCY MARLOW (LOLA LAVERY), HAZEL SHERMET (LIBBY'S SECRETARY), GRADY SUTTON (ARTIE CARVER), FRANK FERGUSON (JUDGE BARNES)

A talented band singer sky-rockets to movie stardom after she meets an alcoholic matinee idol.

This is surely one of the biggest intimate films ever made and a staggering musical and dramatic showcase for Judy Garland. With profoundly moving work by James Mason and director Cukor, *A Star Is Born*, on and off the screen, is a memorably bittersweet experience.

There were musical dramas prior to this one, and star vehicles, but nothing on this scale. For Garland, who had been absent from film for four years, it was a comeback bid to put Norma Desmond in the shade. Garland loved the 1937 film *A Star Is Born* and had played in a radio version, so she and husband Sid Luft conceived an ambitious musical remake. With James Mason as something of an offbeat choice as leading man, the entire project was a far cry from normal musical routine. George Cukor was one of the greatest actors' directors in film, Moss Hart was a superb writer, and Harold Arlen and Ira Gershwin were the best songwriters in the business. Some of what followed might have been predicted: a lengthy shoot marked by delay and illness, an exploding budget, uncertainty from a first-time producer, and finally a film filled with such abundance that its makers let it run over three hours. It opened to outstanding reviews, and the Garland comeback seemed assured, until exhibitors began to complain about its length. Without consulting Cukor, Warner Bros. cut out nearly a half hour, including two major musical numbers. Longer or shorter, it had been too expensive to make a profit, and

when Garland did not win the Academy Award she deserved, the story was pretty much over.

Since the rediscovery of most of its lost footage in the 1980s, the strengths and weaknesses of *A Star Is Born* are now more evident than ever, and largely interdependent: it goes on too long, really, because it's so good. The story would not be so richly meaningful had Cukor and company not taken their time to tell it the way that they did. There is also, built into the story, some fundamental untruth, since it isn't always convincing that a star of Norman's caliber would decline quite this abruptly. Plus, given Garland's extraordinary talent, it may take some doing to believe that Esther is simply a humble unknown. But how good she is! From scene to scene, her approach is as meticulous as Cukor's, and the direct emotion she conveys as a singer is always

"Born in a Trunk"/"Melancholy Baby": Judy Garland

Judy Garland

present, as well, in her acting. "The Man That Got Away," in both performance and staging, is one of the great musical sequences, and the reinstated cut songs offer far more than mere padding. The end of "Lose That Long Face" is a real killer: after breaking down in her dressing room, she dries her tears, paints the freckles back on, and goes out for a brief reprise in a close-up that looks like the comedy and tragedy masks combined.

For many, this is Garland's peak. Others feel her concerts are a purer distillation, and some prefer her younger and less troubled. What cannot be disputed, at any rate, is that *A Star Is Born* is one of the most affecting and most lovingly made of all musicals, a deserved homage to an extraordinary talent.

"Swanee": Judy Garland

Judy Garland and director George Cukor

WHAT'S MORE

The role of Norman Maine was what actors used to call a "plum," yet a number of major leading men turned it down. Doubtless this had to do with apprehension over being sidelined in a take-no-prisoners one-woman show. Among those asked or considered: Humphrey Bogart, Laurence Olivier, Stewart Granger, Frank Sinatra, Richard Burton, and Tyrone Power. The heartbreaker came from Cary Grant, who initially said yes, then quickly withdrew, and who might have been devastating. Let it be reiterated here that Mason is terrific.

• • •

Although the 1983 reconstruction of *Star* was called a restoration, with photographs taking the place of still-lost film, one scene was left behind for lack of sufficient visual material to accompany the recovered soundtrack. As it now runs, Norman simply finds Esther at the Hotel Lancaster; originally, they were swamped by a voracious pack of Maine fans in the lobby. Nancy Kulp, Lauren Chapin, and Barbara Pepper are among those no longer in the film.

MUSICALLY SPEAKING

"Born in a Trunk," the narrated medley Garland performs at the midway point, had not been part of the original concept. It was added after the main shoot finished, when it was decided that the audience needed to see a number that makes Esther a star. Long (fifteen minutes) and stylized in design, it has been both praised and criticized. What fewer dispute is that Garland's performance in much of it—especially "Swanee"—is some of the best work she, or anyone else, ever did.

> ### MORE TO SEE
>
> *Carmen Jones* (1954): Opera via Broadway, with Dorothy Dandridge
>
> *Love Me or Leave Me* (1955): Conflict and stardom with Doris Day and James Cagney

James Mason and Judy Garland

OKLAHOMA!

MAGNA/RKO, 1955 | **COLOR** (TECHNICOLOR)/TODD-AO, 145 MINUTES

DIRECTOR: **FRED ZINNEMANN** PRODUCERS: **ARTHUR HORNBLOW JR.** EXECUTIVE PRODUCERS: **RICHARD RODGERS AND OSCAR HAMMERSTEIN II** SCREENPLAY: **SONYA LEVIEN AND WILLIAM LUDWIG, BASED ON THE MUSICAL PLAY BY OSCAR HAMMERSTEIN II, FROM THE PLAY** *GREEN GROW THE LILACS* BY LYNN RIGGS SONGS: **RICHARD RODGERS (MUSIC) AND OSCAR HAMMERSTEIN II (LYRICS)** CHOREOGRAPHER: **AGNES DE MILLE** STARRING: **GORDON MACRAE (CURLY MCLAIN), SHIRLEY JONES (LAUREY WILLIAMS), GLORIA GRAHAME (ADO ANNIE CARNES), GENE NELSON (WILL PARKER), CHARLOTTE GREENWOOD (AUNT ELLER), EDDIE ALBERT (ALI HAKIM), JAMES WHITMORE (ANDREW CARNES), ROD STEIGER (JUD FRY), BARBARA LAWRENCE (GERTIE CUMMINGS), BAMBI LINN AND JAMES MITCHELL (DREAM LAUREY AND CURLY)**

In the Oklahoma territory, a cowboy and a farmhand vie for the affection of a young woman.

A trailblazer on Broadway in 1943, the first Rodgers and Hammerstein collaboration also marked a turning point in screen musicals. On film, *Oklahoma!* is beautifully cinematic and musically glorious.

Rodgers and Hammerstein had both toiled at film studios, and both had seen fine work get mangled on its way to the screen. Neither was enamored of the motion picture industry, and Hammerstein was so disheartened by his Hollywood experiences that, when he and Rodgers were contracted to write *State Fair* (1945), he stipulated that he would do no work west of his Pennsylvania home. When *Oklahoma!* began its inevitable trip to the screen, Rodgers and Hammerstein shielded it from bad treatment by supervising the production themselves and having it made independently.

Since modern development had transformed the actual Oklahoma landscape, the film was shot in Arizona, mainly around Nogales. A new wide-screen process called Todd-AO

gave the images nearly unprecedented depth and clarity, and between the technology and the location shooting, this was the most expensive musical yet made. With cost and prestige at such an extreme, it was decided to run *Oklahoma!* as a special roadshow attraction, with two-a-day showings at high prices and a slow rollout across the country. This type of presentation soon became the norm for major musicals, and would remain so until the genre declined in the 1970s.

Most musicals benefit from a big screen. *Oklahoma!* virtually demands one, and under ace director Fred Zinnemann, in his only musical, the vistas are magnificent. They also make a subtle and unmistakable case for the show's premise that unspoiled land welcomes the people who want to belong to it. Even before Gordon MacRae launches into "Oh, What a Beautiful Mornin'," Zinnemann's camera has taken a trip through a lush and abundant cornfield that, in Todd-AO, seems to invite viewers to reach out and touch. Between the locations, the cinematography, the dancing, and the musical arrangements, this is one of the most impressive musical productions ever.

It's so abundant, in fact, that sometimes it threatens to dwarf the plot. On the stage, Curly's courting of Laurey seemed urgent, and the dream ballet ("Laurey Makes Up Her Mind") was revolutionary. Here, maybe not as much—singing cowboys had already featured in countless movies, and ballets had propelled the

Top to Bottom | "Pore Jud is Daid": Gordon MacRae and Rod Steiger | Shirley Jones, Gloria Grahame, Eddie Albert | Director Fred Zinnemann and Shirley Jones on the set

plot in films as diverse as *The Red Shoes* and *Cover Girl*. MacRae and Shirley Jones (in a lovely film debut) are fine in the leads, but perhaps lack the charisma of the second couple, the sensational dancer Gene Nelson and the fetchingly eccentric Gloria Grahame. Speaking of odd, there's also Rod Steiger, whose Jud seems to be a refugee from the Actor's Studio. He does very well, however, with his singing chores and even holds up Jud's part of the ballet.

Its astronomical cost made *Oklahoma!* something of a financial disappointment. That situation would be amended with the enormous success of the second Rodgers/Hammerstein/Magna/Todd-AO production, *South Pacific* (1958). While it too was shot on magnificent locations with unusual fidelity to the original show, *Oklahoma!* remains the superior film. Especially when seen on a *really* big screen, it's one of the most impressive of Broadway adaptations, and a great deal more than merely "OK."

"Oh, What a Beautiful Mornin'": Gordon MacRae

Above Gordon MacRae and Charlotte Greenwood
Below Dream Ballet ("Laurey Makes Up Her Mind"): Bambi Linn and James Mitchell

WHAT'S MORE

Surveying what might have been can be both fascinating and peculiar, as the casting of *Oklahoma!* readily proves. Three years before they married, Paul Newman and Joanne Woodward were considered for Curly and Laurie, as were Montgomery Clift and Eva Marie Saint. Both Debbie Reynolds and Mamie Van Doren were possibilities for Ado Annie, while Ernest Borgnine and Eli Wallach were potential Juds. Most arresting was another potential Curly: James Dean tested for the role by performing "Pore Jud" with Steiger. His acting was fine but his singing was judged insufficiently strong. Just imagine.

• • •

Most theaters were not equipped to handle Todd-AO, which was not compatible with other formats. The solution was to film every scene in 70mm Todd-AO and again in 35mm CinemaScope, which was available virtually everywhere by 1955. The latter was the version far more people saw, and the one first shown on television. The two have numerous differences in movements and line readings, as well as different opening credits. Both are available in home video formats, so see (and hear) for yourself.

MUSICALLY SPEAKING

Gloria Grahame was an accomplished, Oscar-winning actress, but not a singer. To get her through Ado Annie's songs, it was necessary to record her doing both "I Cain't Say No" and "All 'er Nothin'" many times, then piece together renditions out of tiny aural bits, and sometimes just individual words and notes. It made for painstakingly hard work, and it was worth it: the recordings sound seamless, and Grahame's Annie all but steals the film.

MORE TO SEE

Carousel (1956): More Rodgers/Hammerstein, Jones/MacRae, and grand location photography

1776 (1972): A later Broadway hit, another faithful filming

Top   "The Surrey with the Fringe on Top": Gordon MacRae and Shirley Jones | **Bottom** "People Will Say We're in Love": Gordon MacRae and Shirley Jones

THE KING AND I

TWENTIETH CENTURY-FOX, 1956 | COLOR (DELUXE)/CINEMASCOPE 55, 133 MINUTES

DIRECTOR: WALTER LANG   PRODUCER: CHARLES BRACKETT   SCREENPLAY: ERNEST LEHMAN, BASED ON THE MUSICAL PLAY BY OSCAR HAMMERSTEIN II, FROM THE BOOK *ANNA AND THE KING OF SIAM* BY MARGARET LANDON   SONGS: RICHARD RODGERS (MUSIC) AND OSCAR HAMMERSTEIN II (LYRICS)   CHOREOGRAPHER: JEROME ROBBINS   STARRING: DEBORAH KERR (ANNA LEONOWENS), YUL BRYNNER (KING MONGKUT OF SIAM), RITA MORENO (TUPTIM), MARTIN BENSON (KRALAHOME), TERRY SAUNDERS (LADY THIANG), REX THOMPSON (LOUIS LEONOWENS), CARLOS RIVAS (LUN THA), PATRICK ADIARTE (PRINCE CHULALONGKORN), YURIKO (ELIZA)

Cultures clash when a British widow travels to Bangkok to serve as school-teacher to the children of the King of Siam.

R arely in a musical does conflict take precedence over romance. It does here, and works as well on film as on the stage. For this, much credit must go to a peerless star duo, a magnificent ballet, and some of Rodgers and Hammerstein's greatest songs.

The King and I has been so loved for so long that it's easy to forget a couple of key points. One is that the real Anna Leonowens was never as great an influence on King Mongkut of Siam (now Thailand) as she claimed. The other is that the musical derives far less from its credited

Deborah Kerr and Yul Brynner

source material, Margaret Landon's book *Anna and the King of Siam* (based on Leonowens's original books), than from the 1946 film with Irene Dunne and Rex Harrison. For that version, Landon's rambling narrative was made more concise and a minor character, Tuptim, elevated in importance. It was theater legend Gertrude Lawrence who, after seeing the film, envisioned it as a musical and, for her, an ideal vehicle. In the hands of Rodgers and Hammerstein, it became far greater, and as played by the all-but-unknown Yul Brynner, the role of the King became equal to that of Anna. Lawrence died during the Broadway run, Brynner repeated his role on film, and *The King and I* quickly became one of the largest grossers in Twentieth Century-Fox history. His Academy Award for the role ensured that Brynner's stamp would long remain on the King, and he later returned to the stage to play thousands of performances of *The King and I* virtually until the end of his life.

Where some movie musicals blossom under the leadership of a great director, *The King and I* is gifted with a cast, script, and score so strong that not even run-of-the-mill direction can defeat them. Walter Lang was an old hand at Fox musicals, competent if rarely inspired, which in this case was preferable to a hands-on approach by someone with wrongheaded notions. While the subsidiary love story has been reduced, the stage show has, by and large, been greatly respected. The sets and costumes are breathtaking, as are the orchestral arrangements by Alfred Newman, and profound gratitude to whoever decided to retain the "Small House of Uncle Thomas" ballet

and its creator, Jerome Robbins. In a lesser film, such an imaginative presentation might overwhelm everything else; here, it fits in beautifully with that stunning group of songs and the star performances. Who can forget "I Whistle a Happy Tune," "Getting to Know You," "Hello, Young Lovers"? And who could deny that, as staged by Robbins, "Shall We Dance?" is one of the great song-and-dance duets of all time? As for Kerr and Brynner, they play out all the facets—the attraction under the hostility, the head-to-head conflict, the cultural clash—with a passion and forcefulness that are rarely witnessed in musical cinema or anywhere else.

The people of Thailand have not been happy with *The King and I*, particularly with the way their king, culture, and faith are portrayed as, in some ways, barbaric. That's an important topic, if for another discussion. (There was also an animated remake in 1999, a fact which many may not remember.) What matters most here is that *The King and I* is a beloved show and became a terrific movie.

Top to Bottom "Getting to Know You": Rita Moreno (f
left), Deborah Kerr, Terry Saunders | Yul Brynner
Rita Moreno (back to camera), Yul Brynner, Debor
Kerr

WHAT'S MORE

Nineteen-fifty-six was certainly Yul Brynner's year, moviewise. He had been cast as Pharaoh in *The Ten Commandments* while still performing the King on Broadway, and these two films plus a third, *Anastasia*, made for one of those acting Oscar wins that was a foregone conclusion. Unfortunately, a longtime addiction to smoking was already compromising his health: Deborah Kerr later recalled that during "Shall We Dance?," Brynner's oxygen tank was always close at hand.

• • •

The role of Tuptim was originally cast with Dorothy Dandridge, in what was to be her first film after the sensational *Carmen Jones*. Dandridge, however, was enamored of neither the role nor its servile overtones, and after walking out was replaced by Rita Moreno. Dandridge's reasons for the turndown are completely understandable, although surely for many artists this would be a difficult choice to make. (Even if secondary and problematic, it was still a high-profile role in a very important movie.) Tuptim, who has less to do in the film than she did on the stage, does not really possess the standout qualities of Dandridge's Carmen Jones—or, for that matter, Moreno's Anita in *West Side Story*.

MUSICALLY SPEAKING

Maureen O'Hara, whose excellent singing voice had been little heard in films, was a possibility for the role of Anna until Richard Rodgers called her a "pirate queen" because of her swashbuckling movie roles. Deborah Kerr, who was more prestigious if not a singer, worked closely with Marni Nixon to achieve a seamless blend of speech (Kerr) and song (Nixon), and it's probably the greatest single job of voice-dubbing ever. Another young vocalist, Marilyn Horne, was runner-up to Nixon to supply Anna's voice. With her operatic superstardom still a few years away, she made it into the film as one of the off-screen singers in "Uncle Thomas."

MORE TO SEE

Guys and Dolls (1955): Broadway's hit, starring a game Marlon Brando and a terrific Jean Simmons

Flower Drum Song (1961): Lesser, but still enjoyable Rodgers and Hammerstein

---

"Shall We Dance?": Yul Brynner and Deborah Kerr

THE GIRL CAN'T HELP IT

TWENTIETH CENTURY-FOX, 1956 | COLOR (DELUXE)/CINEMASCOPE, 99 MINUTES

DIRECTOR AND PRODUCER: FRANK TASHLIN   SCREENPLAY: FRANK TASHLIN AND HERBERT BAKER, BASED ON THE NOVEL *DO RE MI* BY GARSON KANIN   SONGS: BOBBY TROUP, FATS DOMINO, GENE VINCENT, AND OTHERS   STARRING: TOM EWELL (TOM MILLER), JAYNE MANSFIELD (JERI JORDAN), EDMOND O'BRIEN (MARTIN "FATS" MURDOCK), HENRY JONES (MOUSIE), JUANITA MOORE (HILDA), AS THEMSELVES: JULIE LONDON, FATS DOMINO, LITTLE RICHARD, RAY ANTHONY, THE PLATTERS, EDDIE COCHRAN, GENE VINCENT, ABBEY LINCOLN, THE TRENIERS, NINO TEMPO, THE CHUCKLES

An ex-con hires a washed-up press agent to turn his talent-free girl-friend into a singing star.

The earliest movies to feature rock 'n' roll artists were ramshackle and cheap, with one exception. This gaudy mashup of rock and Jayne Mansfield is a historical document, a cinematic jukebox, and a riot.

Film first acknowledged rock 'n' roll when MGM's *The Blackboard Jungle* began, startlingly, with the sounds of "Rock Around the Clock." Then, in 1956, Bill Haley and the Comets starred in two movies and disc jockey Alan Freed, the "Father of Rock 'n' Roll," appeared in three. Twentieth Century-Fox was already planning *The Girl Can't Help It* as a vehicle for a new star, Jayne Mansfield, and quickly reconfigured it for Mansfield to share the screen and the soundtrack with a large assortment of rock and pop artists. (Fox certainly covered its musical bases that year: traditional fare like *The King and I* and *Carousel*, plus this and Elvis Presley's first film, *Love Me Tender*.) The result was a box-office hit at a time when most studios were leery of rock, and the presence of such artists as

Little Richard, Fats Domino, and the Platters indicated that the complexion of pop music and culture was changing, along with the sound.

Without Frank Tashlin, *The Girl Can't Help It* might have been a hopeless jumble of comedy and guest stars. Tashlin had made animated films before moving on to live action, and instead of treating Mansfield like a carbon-copy Marilyn, Tashlin treats her, essentially, like a character in one of his cartoons. Mansfield leans forward while she walks, all but knocks over furniture when making sharp turns, and then there's that famous shot of her holding up two bottles of milk. She comes in contact with rock 'n' roll only intermittently, most conspicuously when Geri records "Rock Around the Rock Pile" and shows that her main talent is not being a siren but sounding like one. With all this, it's to Mansfield's credit that she is able to convey that there's a sweet young woman underneath all the sequins and brouhaha.

In the crooked and sometimes insane music business portrayed here, rock 'n' roll is definitely the new world order, and the artists are treated with respect. In contrast with the flat monochrome of other early rock movies, Tashlin's cartoonist eye makes them pop: Little Richard, with his silver-tipped shoes and shiny suit, is as striking to look at as to listen to, and his two songs, the title number and "She's Got It," are testaments to his talent as well as wry comments on Mansfield herself. If she and the

"Be-Bop-a-Lula": Gene Vincent and his Blue Caps

rock artists do not necessarily operate on the same wavelength, the movie's witty prologue has already pointed out that the world is changing, and fast. Clearly, the singers are all okay with the furor they're causing, and some of them, like Domino, Little Richard, and the Platters, kept going for a long time. Others flashed and vanished (the Chuckles), and a few died way too young, like Eddie Cochran and Gene Vincent, plus Mansfield herself. Here, they're all young and vital and in peak form, and this giddy satire of fame, stardom, and the music business is a dandy way for a movie to salute their talent. Just don't expect its director to take them—or anything—too seriously.

WHAT'S MORE

While its depiction of the music business as a crime-ridden snake pit seems to be a typical Tashlin exaggeration, this film was being quite prescient. By 1960, the music industry was awash in a series of scandals over payola, now commonly known (in entertainment and politics) as "pay to play." The once-mighty career of Alan Freed collapsed after he was charged with conflict-of-interest and bribery, and the up-and-coming Dick Clark narrowly avoided something similar.

• • •

Edmond O'Brien, Jayne Mansfield, Tom Ewell

One of the supposed ironies in *The Girl Can't Help It* is that though Jayne Mansfield is believed to be tone-deaf, she actually can sing. It's obvious, however, that Jeri's "voice" near the end isn't Mansfield's. It belongs to Eileen Wilson, who often served in this capacity. Later, in *The Sheriff of Fractured Jaw*, Mansfield would be dubbed by none other than pop queen Connie Francis. While she sang for herself in nightclubs and made several recordings, vocalism was never Mansfield's forte. She did, on occasion, play the violin—a touch which might have made this movie even nuttier.

MUSICALLY SPEAKING

One of the most arresting moments here, and a neat break from all the up-tempo music and comedy, comes when a drunken Tom Ewell is haunted by the recurring specter of Julie London singing "Cry Me a River." With its striking use of color and procession of gorgeous gowns (seven), the sequence looks as sultry as it sounds. It also serves as a reminder that Ms. London's handlers paid almost as much attention to her album covers as to her vocals. Her movie career was erratic, and this scene hints at some good things that, on film, never really happened.

> ### MORE TO SEE
>
> *The Big Broadcast* (1932): Pop music and guest stars from an earlier era
>
> *Phantom of the Paradise* (1974): Music, satire, and horror

Tom Ewell, Edmond O'Brien, Jayne Mansfield, Henry Jones

FUNNY FACE

PARAMOUNT, 1957 | COLOR (TECHNICOLOR)/VISTAVISION, 103 MINUTES

DIRECTOR: **STANLEY DONEN**   PRODUCER: **ROGER EDENS**   SCREENPLAY: **LEONARD GERSHE**   SONGS: **GEORGE GERSHWIN (MUSIC) AND IRA GERSHWIN (LYRICS)**   CHOREOGRAPHERS: **FRED ASTAIRE AND EUGENE LORING**   STARRING: **AUDREY HEPBURN (JO STOCKTON), FRED ASTAIRE (DICK AVERY), KAY THOMPSON (MAGGIE PRESCOTT), MICHEL AUCLAIR (PROFESSOR EMILE FLOSTRE), ROBERT FLEMYNG (PAUL DUVAL), DOVIMA (MARION), SUZY PARKER AND SUNNY HARTNETT (MODELS), VIRGINIA GIBSON (BABS), SUE ENGLAND (LAURA), RUTA LEE (LETTIE)**

A fashion photographer discovers his latest model in a Greenwich Village bookstore and takes her to Paris for a shoot.

C
hic" doesn't begin to describe it. This gleaming entertainment is a love letter to Paris and probably the greatest fashion show of all time.

Essentially, *Funny Face* is an MGM musical made at Paramount, displaying the production style of one studio under the auspices of another. This came about because Audrey Hepburn was under contract to Paramount, wanted to star in a musical being planned at MGM, and Paramount would not consent to a loan-out. (In the big-studio days, the presence of a major star could take precedence over a whole team of production personnel.) The title and some of the songs were from a 1926 Gershwin show that had starred Fred Astaire, and Astaire and Hepburn played roles based on superstar photographer Richard Avedon and his first wife.

"Basal Metabolism": Fred Astaire and Audrey Hepburn

Arranger and cabaret stylist Kay Thompson costarred as a character modeled after *Vogue* editor Diana Vreeland, while Avedon himself served as a technical advisor and oversaw the innovative use of color. As much of the production as possible was shot in and around Paris, to glorious effect and to the irritation of some sour-tempered Parisian authorities, who found the work disruptive. The result was captivating and well reviewed, and also a major box-office disappointment. Paramount did get some further return with a 1964 reissue timed to cash in on that other Hepburn musical, *My Fair Lady*.

Funny Face is composed of any number of exquisite components: Gershwin music, Avedon's marvelous color-separation visuals, ultra-smooth direction by Donen, a witty screenplay, Hepburn and Astaire offering variations on the term "star charisma," and Givenchy fashions so timeless that most could be worn today. The musical numbers (most of them) are choice, beginning with Thompson's ultra-crisp

"Think Pink!" and on to Hepburn's delicately wistful "How Long Has This Been Going On?," the ebullient "Bonjour, Paris!," and Astaire turning "Let's Kiss and Make Up" into a giddy bullfight dance. The grand duet "He Loves and She Loves" is beautifully shot through diffused filters in the French countryside, though some have noted that Hepburn's dance skills may not quite be up to Astaire's. There can, in fact, be some comment about the whole of *Funny Face* not ultimately being as great as those wonderful parts. The spoof of French intellectualism, in particular, seems somewhat narrow and mean-spirited, and Thompson, expert as she is, portrays a character so brittle as to sometimes seem incapable of human feeling. Fortunately, Astaire is as virtuosic as ever, Hepburn has infinite reserves of charm and appeal, and they work well together as a pair. Best of all, there is that fashion-shoot montage that seems to cover all of Paris and climaxes with Hepburn's dazzling red-draped descent down the Louvre stairs in

Left "Think Pink!": Kay Thompson | **Right** Audrey Hepburn

front of the *Winged Victory of Samothrace*. Other movies may have glamour and excitement, but this scene stands alone.

Years before anyone used the term "supermodel," *Funny Face* gave the fashion industry both some affectionate tweaking and a glorious depiction. In Hepburn, it had a star who really could be a superstar model, just as Astaire might pass for a celebrated photog and Thompson a doyenne of style. It's a musical for connoisseurs, an unsurpassable delight for those willing and eager to yield to its spell. That, even without those gowns, is plenty.

"Bonjour, Paris": Kay Thompson, Fred Astaire, Audrey Hepburn

"He Loves and She Loves": Audrey Hepburn and Fred Astaire

WHAT'S MORE

The "inside fashion" vibe in *Funny Face* was given even more credibility by the on-screen presence of three of the decade's leading models. Suzy Parker and Sunny Hartnett appear in "Think Pink!," and Dovima, one of Avedon's best-known muses, plays Astaire's model in the bookstore, who is intently reading a comic book. Lest anyone think that this detail was intended as a put-down, be advised that in real life Dovima was so wild about comics that she once traveled to an overseas assignment with a trunk completely filled with them.

• • •

Since fretting was second nature to Astaire, he naturally found things to rile him during the shoot. One was the thirty-year age difference between himself and Hepburn, which has indeed not always sat well with viewers. Hepburn, for her part, feared she could not keep up with the master in their dances together. Fortunately, these two professionals found a central meeting point, as Stanley Donen noted in a tribute to Hepburn after her death. "Fred would assure Audrey that she was a wonderful dance partner," he wrote, "and she would assure him that he was not too old for her. What held it together was that both thought the other was near perfection."

MUSICALLY SPEAKING

In the "Basal Metabolism" dance, set to Gershwin melodies and choreographed by Eugene Loring, Hepburn appears to be the epitome of elfin cool. This belies her inner turmoil over one item of costuming: she absolutely loathed wearing white socks with an otherwise black ensemble. Donen, knowing how Astaire and Kelly wore them to make an audience focus on their feet, insisted on white. Hepburn, who was self-conscious about the size of her feet, wanted black. Finally, if in anguish, she did it his way, and after seeing the number she admitted that he'd been right.

MORE TO SEE

Silk Stockings (1957): Astaire, with Cole Porter songs

Finian's Rainbow (1968): Astaire, directed by Francis Ford Coppola

Opposite Audrey Hepburn and Dovima
Right "Clap Yo' Hands": Fred Astaire and Kay Thompson

THE PAJAMA GAME

WARNER BROS., 1957 | COLOR (WARNERCOLOR), 101 MINUTES

DIRECTORS AND PRODUCERS: GEORGE ABBOTT AND STANLEY DONEN   SCREENPLAY: GEORGE ABBOTT AND RICHARD BISSELL, BASED ON THEIR MUSICAL PLAY, FROM BISSELL'S NOVEL *7½ CENTS*   SONGS: RICHARD ADLER AND JERRY ROSS   CHOREOGRAPHER: BOB FOSSE   STARRING: DORIS DAY (KATIE "BABE" WILLIAMS), JOHN RAITT (SID SOROKIN), CAROL HANEY (GLADYS HOTCHKISS), EDDIE FOY JR. (VERNON HINES), RETA SHAW (MABEL), BARBARA NICHOLS (POOPSIE), THELMA PELISH (MAE), JACK STRAW (PREZ), RALPH DUNN (MYRON HASLER), BUZZ MILLER AND KENNETH LEROY (DANCERS)

The new superintendent at a Midwestern pajama factory collides with, then romances, the head of the grievance committee.

Strange but true: a musical about a labor-versus-management struggle wound up as a Broadway smash and an exceptionally good film. For those seeking an ideal middle-of-the-road way to turn a show into a movie, have a look at this one.

Without being especially innovative, *The Pajama Game* was a near-perfect show for the mid-1950s. It had a believable plot, mostly engaging characters, songs that could fit the story yet stand alone, and swell choreography by Bob Fosse. All of those things made the trip to Hollywood (Burbank, actually), along with the Broadway director, George Abbott, and most of the original cast. The most conspicuous cast change was, in this case, a crucial factor. On the stage, Janis Paige had played the lead with guts, great timing, and a so-so singing voice. On film it was Doris Day, an outstanding singer who also possessed everything else the role needed.

Abbott, for his part, entered into a codirecting setup with film pro Stanley Donen, which meant that Donen essentially directed the film with occasional suggestions and comments from Abbott. This, for Donen, was a far more compatible situation than the occasionally tense times when he shared the director's chair with Gene Kelly. The result was a version of the show slightly shortened (some songs and a ballet cut) and also skillfully opened up and subtly

deepened. The one downside concerned some historical currents. Movie musicals had begun their split between the big Broadway blockbusters like *South Pacific* and the low-budget items with of-the-moment pop stars. A moderately sized item like *The Pajama Game* could not, for all its merit, fit in to such an equation, and its box-office performance was held to be a disappointment. Neither Day nor Donen made many more musicals.

While *The Pajama Game* did not initially get the reception it deserved, there is nothing about it that isn't buoyant, joyous, and completely delightful. This wasn't a show that needed to be blown up for movies, nor outfitted with gimmicks, and the atmosphere is as realistic as

Doris Day, John Raitt, Carol Haney

the subject demands, with more stylization for sequences like "Hernando's Hideaway." With the casting of Day, the material acquired a depth that it had not really had on the stage. She was, by this point, as insightful and intuitive an actor as any working in film, and she inhabits the role so completely that a viewer can only be elated by her work, if regretful that she so seldom had opportunities like this and *Calamity Jane*. Raitt is every inch and decibel a fine leading man, and if Carol Haney relies too much on mugging in her comedy scenes, she's pretty divine in "Steam Heat" and the other dance numbers. There is also, dance-wise, the fun of watching the bountiful Reta Shaw do a deft soft shoe with Eddie

Foy Jr. Without any vocal dubbing, the cast does full justice to the show's main hit, "Hey There," and to all the other songs in this infectious score.

Donen and Abbott followed this with the film of the only other show written by Richard Adler and Jerry Ross, *Damn Yankees*. Again there was unusual fidelity to the material, and once more a movie name (Tab Hunter) came in for one of the leads. There were some terrific moments, but it was a more uneven show on the stage, and baseball did not seem quite as compelling on film as life in a garment factory. *The Pajama Game* remains the winner, and a musical to enjoy over and over.

"Once-a-Year Day": Carol Haney

WHAT'S MORE

For stage stalwart John Raitt, this would be his one film role of any real size. Originally, Warners had thought of Frank Sinatra, who turned it down, and then Bing Crosby, who wanted too much money. Abbott favored Marlon Brando, despite his rather controversial performance in *Guys and Dolls*. Day, for her part, wanted Dean Martin. Finally, Raitt made one screen test on the East Coast and another in California with Day, and wound up pleasing everyone.

• • •

Two main assets of the film are its swift pace and its modestly scaled production, both of which came from making virtue out of necessity. According to Donen, the studio had so little belief in the project that it "didn't care if it got made or not." Consequently, there were no frills and a shooting schedule so rushed that, as Raitt later quipped, "I never had time to sit in the canvas chair that had my name on it."

MUSICALLY SPEAKING

With musicals venturing increasingly off the soundstage and out into the world, it was an easy decision for Donen and Fosse to spend a week shooting "Once-a-Year Day" in Hollenbeck and Griffith Parks in Los Angeles. With Haney, other cast members, and eighty dancers, this sequence is a perfect summation of why this movie works: it's creative, filled with bright-colored exuberance, and just plain fun.

> ### MORE TO SEE
>
> *Damn Yankees* (1958): Not as good as this, yet a chance to see Gwen Verdon in action
>
> *Hello, Dolly!* (1969): Making a Broadway show *way* too big, with diverting moments

Left "7½ Cents": Jack Straw, Barbara Nichols, Thelma Pelish, Doris Day
Right "There Once Was a Man": Doris Day and John Raitt

JAILHOUSE ROCK

MGM, 1957 | BLACK AND WHITE/CINEMASCOPE, 96 MINUTES

DIRECTOR: RICHARD THORPE   PRODUCER: PANDRO S. BERMAN   SCREENPLAY: GUY TROSPER, BASED ON THE STORY BY NED YOUNG   SONGS: JERRY LEIBER AND MIKE STOLLER, AARON SCHROEDER AND BEN WEISMAN   CHOREOGRAPHER: ALEX ROMERO (UNCREDITED)   STARRING: ELVIS PRESLEY (VINCE EVERETT), JUDY TYLER (PEGGY VAN ALDEN), MICKEY SHAUGHNESSY (HUNK HOUGHTON), VAUGHN TAYLOR (MR. SHORES), JENNIFER HOLDEN (SHERRY WILSON), DEAN JONES (TEDDY TALBOT), ANNE NEYLAND (LAURY JACKSON), GRANDON RHODES (PROFESSOR VAN ALDEN), KATHERINE WARREN (MRS. VAN ALDEN)

After serving jail time for manslaughter, a young man becomes a rock star.

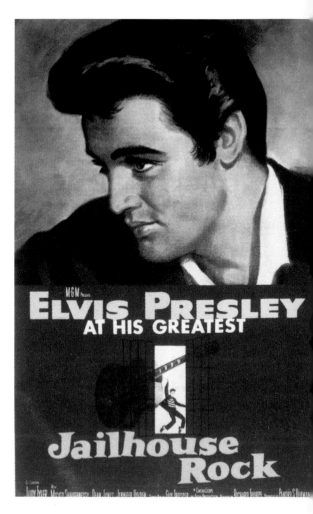

It's as much of a star vehicle as *A Star Is Born* and a time capsule equal to *The Girl Can't Help It*. It has edge and spark to spare, most of it in the person of a major new musical figure: Elvis. He was a natural on film—photogenic and assured, with a slight James Dean vibe, excellent instincts about how to move and speak, and an effortless projection of raw sexuality. This was made clear in his first movie, *Love Me Tender* (1956), it was obvious in his second, *Loving You* (1957), and it's completely unavoidable in his third, *Jailhouse Rock*.

What, after all, could better suit Elvis's bad-boy persona than to cast him as a surly ex-con-turned-rock-idol? With fight scenes, love scenes, prison torture, and frequent song interludes, there was plenty of the Elvis that

"Baby I Don't Care": Elvis Presley

fans adored and parents feared. Added to that was possibly the single most essential sequence of his career: that indelible Leiber/Stoller title song, with its driving beat and its oddly appropriate "Old meets New Hollywood" staging. The black-and-white photography helped as well, evoking mood, danger, and immediacy instead of movieland gloss. Along with Elvis's next film, *King Creole* (1958)—his last film in black and white—*Jailhouse Rock* is pretty hot testimony to who Elvis was, and why he became famous.

In the canon of essential musicals, *Jailhouse Rock* occupies a double-edged position. On the one hand, it's the ultimate document of Elvis in his young, sensational prime. Also, more poignantly, it seems to announce a movie career more substantial than the one that actually followed. *Jailhouse Rock* and *King Creole* could and even should have been the beginning of great things—but then Elvis was drafted, and after he returned from the army much of the raw power was gone. Both his look and his sound had become glossier and less threatening, and the energy of *Jailhouse Rock* eventually dissipated into such uninspired fare as *Harum Scarum* and *Tickle Me* (both 1965). While the films continued to be profitable, especially in the South, there was rarely that of-the-moment kind of excitement so evident in Elvis's earliest roles. Two later titles bear interest specifically because they were musicals: *Frankie and Johnny* (1966) could have been made at Twentieth Century-Fox in the 1940s with Dan Dailey and possibly Betty Grable. In a somewhat creaky, old-fashioned way, it at least tried to connect Elvis with the traditions of musical cinema. More spectacularly, *Viva Las Vegas* (1964) is favored by Elvis buffs because of his high-octane meeting with Ann-Margret. The potent commingling of star power is irresistible and, like *Jailhouse Rock*, hints at other paths in other movies. Such things were not to be, however—which is why the legend of Elvis encompasses both great achievement and some major potential that was short-circuited.

Jailhouse Rock, then, is a beacon in Elvis's movie career. Even with some clichés and direction that doesn't always match its star's dynamism, it moves and often crackles. Crucially, and unlike some of the later Elvis titles, it is self-evidently a genuine product and reflection of its time. Among all his movies, *Jailhouse Rock* is the one that best demonstrates that Elvis didn't only have the stuff on recordings and in live performance: he had it on film, too. It's all up there, in beautiful black and white and CinemaScope, for everyone to see.

Above Mickey Shaughnessy and Elvis Presley
Below "Jailhouse Rock": Elvis Presley

Judy Tyler and Elvis Presley on the set

Top Hugh Sanders (left) and Elvis Presley | **Bottom** Shooting the title song

WHAT'S MORE

Judy Tyler's assertive screen presence makes her quite unlike other young women who played opposite Elvis. She had appeared on Broadway in the Rodgers and Hammerstein show *Pipe Dream* and, quite clearly, was on her way to bigger things. What a tragedy, then, that she and her husband were killed in an auto accident just three weeks after she finished working on *Jailhouse Rock*. She was only twenty-four. It's said that Elvis took her death so hard that he was never able to watch the film; what's incontestable is that a promising career was ended far, far too early.

• • •

Elvis's films were seldom (or never) noted for their budgetary largesse. It was very telling, in the 1960s, that two of the King's most paltry vehicles, *Kissin' Cousins* (1964) and *Harum Scarum*, were produced by the notoriously chintzy "King of the Bs," Sam Katzman. For such as these, the only major item on the budget would be Elvis's salary. *Jailhouse Rock* was not in that league, nor as inexpensive as has sometimes been stated. Its $1.1 million cost was average for a mid-range MGM production at the time, and it gave the studio a major profit at a time when most of its musicals (like *Silk Stockings* and *Les Girls*) were tallying huge losses.

MUSICALLY SPEAKING

It goes without saying that the title number is what people remember most about *Jailhouse Rock*. The song, the setting, and Elvis's moves (which he "choreographed" himself) are so indelible that the other songs he performs tend to get erased. "Young and Beautiful" is favored by some fans, but the real keeper is "Treat Me Nice"—as definitive a song and rendition as he would ever do.

> ### MORE TO SEE
>
> *Viva Las Vegas* (1964): Elvis and Ann-Margret, striking sparks
>
> *Jesus Christ Superstar* (1972): The quintessential rock opera

Elvis Presley and Judy Tyler

GIGI

MGM, 1958 | COLOR (METROCOLOR)/CINEMASCOPE, 115 MINUTES

DIRECTOR: VINCENTE MINNELLI   PRODUCER: ARTHUR FREED   SCREENPLAY: ALAN JAY LERNER, BASED ON THE NOVELLA BY COLETTE   SONGS: FREDERICK LOEWE (MUSIC) AND ALAN JAY LERNER (LYRICS)   STARRING: LESLIE CARON (GIGI), MAURICE CHEVALIER (HONORÉ LACHAILLE), LOUIS JOURDAN (GASTON LACHAILLE), HERMIONE GINGOLD (MADAME ALVAREZ), EVA GABOR (LIANE D'EXELMANS), JACQUES BERGERAC (SANDOMIR), ISABEL JEANS (AUNT ALICIA), JOHN ABBOTT (MANUEL)

A turn-of-the-century Parisian gamine is groomed to be the mistress of a wealthy young playboy.

Whether or not it's the greatest, *Gigi* represents a kind of thrilling culmination of one cornerstone of the movie musical: the MGM productions of Arthur Freed. It's a long path from *The Broadway Melody* to *Gigi*, and Freed was there the whole time. For him and for Vincente Minnelli, *Gigi* was a joyful climax, with a truckload of Academy Awards as the icing on the cake. Both sweet and roguish, *Gigi* remains a tasty and supremely elegant soufflé of delight, proof once again that it takes an enormous amount of toil to produce something that can appear this effortless.

Contrary to some notions, *Gigi* was not MGM's answer, with a French accent, to *My Fair Lady*. The original Colette novella had been published in 1944, filmed in France in 1949, and two years later became a non-musical Broadway play starring a young Audrey Hepburn. That was when Freed began to think about it as a possible musical, with censorship as the main

obstacle: in the Eisenhower era, the notion of training a mistress seemed completely immoral. Ultimately, Freed won clearance by assuring the Production Code Administration that making *Gigi* a musical would soften the plot's harsher edges. *My Fair Lady* had opened by this time, and Freed engaged its key personnel—Lerner, Loewe, and designer Cecil Beaton. Another defining choice came with Freed's contention that a studio mockup could never compare with genuine Parisian locations. Here, Maxim's and the Jardin des Tuileries and the Palais de Glace are all real, and a long way from the *faux-français* soundstage of *An American in Paris*.

Gigi displays many kinds of perfection: an ideal cast, the score, Beaton's designs, and Minnelli's unerring instincts for where to put the camera and how to stage the action. There is also, in a larger sense, the rightness of its place in the musical film continuum. Like *Singin' in the Rain*, it compels the musical's past and present to come together in a grand duet of tradition, skill, and joy. This is most evident with the participation of Maurice Chevalier. He had been there at

Top Leslie Caron and Isabel Jeans | **Bottom** "I'm Glad I'm Not Young Anymore": Maurice Chevalier

the dawn of movie musicals and, nearly thirty years later, was still (say it with its French pronunciation) formidable. From "Thank Heaven for Little Girls" on, he is the warm and wise anchor for all the action—Lerner's benevolent Greek chorus. "I Remember It Well" is almost overwhelming in its wistful resonance and, late in the proceedings, he has an irresistible chance to sum up his career and even take a bow. To conclude "I'm Glad I'm Not Young Anymore," he takes out his trademark straw hat and exits the screen doing the same music hall strut that had been delighting audiences for fifty years.

In one sublime and joyous moment, *Gigi* and Chevalier allow us to see the entire history of the movie musical, past, present, and even future.

The rightness of much of *Gigi* is just enough to remind us that no, it's not entirely ideal. Some will wish for more dancing, the wit can occasionally seem calculated, and some modern viewers may take issue with some of the story's undertones. Still, even a moment or two of unease shouldn't mar the brilliant and graceful remainder. The happy fact is that *Gigi* remains as much of a charmer as she ever was, and always worthy of another champagne toast.

Leslie Caron

WHAT'S MORE

The Paris authorities felt that previous movie companies coming to their city had been obtrusive, destructive, and traffic snarling, and they were far from happy that the *Gigi* crew planned to cut a wide swath through the City of Light. Consequently, they made sure that Minnelli and his associates were kept on a tight rein. The shoot at Maxim's was especially nerve-racking, yet, due to meticulous organization and some luck, it all ended up without major material or human casualties.

• • •

Leslie Caron had sung in her previous four-letter MGM hit, *Lili*, and originally believed she'd be singing Gigi's songs as well. As with other stars before and after her, it ended up otherwise, with Caron's songs dubbed by Betty Wand. The original tracks made by Caron survive and her version of "The Parisians" is especially delightful.

MUSICALLY SPEAKING

"Say a Prayer for Me Tonight" was originally written for *My Fair Lady* and sung by Eliza before the Embassy Ball. Cut during the show's out-of-town tryout, it was exhumed by Lerner and Loewe and given to Caron/Wand. Not unexpectedly, *Gigi*'s songs drew criticism in some quarters for being inferior copies of those in *Fair Lady*. The title song, in particular, was alleged to be a clone of "I've Grown Accustomed to Her Face." Not true, not fair, and *Salut!* to Lerner and Loewe.

> MORE TO SEE
>
> *The Merry Widow* (1934): Chevalier, Jeanette MacDonald, and Lubitsch at MGM
>
> *The Tales of Hoffmann* (1951): Stylish and operatic, via director Michael Powell

Leslie Caron, Maurice Chevalier, Hermione Gingold, Louis Jourdan

Louis Jourdan and Eva Gabor

WEST SIDE STORY

MIRISCH CORPORATION/UNITED ARTISTS, 1961 | COLOR (TECHNICOLOR)/ SUPER PANAVISION 70, 152 MINUTES

DIRECTORS: ROBERT WISE AND JEROME ROBBINS   PRODUCER: ROBERT WISE   SCREENPLAY: ERNEST LEHMAN, BASED ON THE MUSICAL PLAY BY ARTHUR LAURENTS   SONGS: LEONARD BERNSTEIN (MUSIC) AND STEPHEN SONDHEIM (LYRICS) CHOREOGRAPHER: JEROME ROBBINS   STARRING: NATALIE WOOD (MARIA), RICHARD BEYMER (TONY), RUSS TAMBLYN (RIFF), RITA MORENO (ANITA), GEORGE CHAKIRIS (BERNARDO), SIMON OAKLAND (SCHRANK), NED GLASS (DOC), WILLIAM BRAMLEY (KRUPKE), TUCKER SMITH (ICE), TONY MORDENTE (ACTION)

A boy and a girl meet and fall in love against a background of prejudice and gang violence.

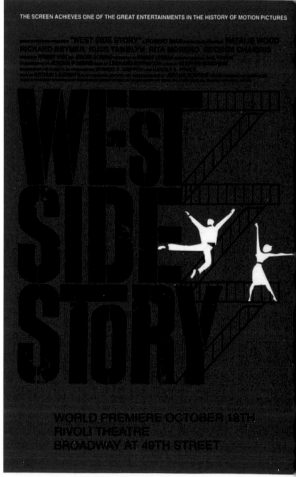

Among the many Broadway shows that have also been part of the film equation, *West Side Story* is a special, stand-apart case. In its urgent subject matter and history-making dance, in its updating of *Romeo and Juliet* and its gloriously varied score by Leonard Bernstein, the show was both a milestone and, for filmmakers, a challenge. To say that it was successfully transferred to the screen is an understatement: this was an "event" in a way few movie musicals had ever been. Even apart from its ten Academy Awards, it remains, for many, a touchstone of the musical form, one of the times the movies really got it right.

From its first seconds, *West Side Story* is electrifyingly unlike other musicals and other movies. After Bernstein's rich overture, there is an aerial panorama of Manhattan, with a series of overhead shots moving in, finally, to a basketball court on a playground. With finger-snapping and some jazzy Bernstein sounds, the action starts with a group of Anglo gang members, asserting their ownership in joyful dance moves. Then they meet the enemy: members of a rival gang, this one Puerto Rican. They skirmish and, until the police arrive, the entire story is told solely through music and dance. Plus, wondrously, it has been filmed not on soundstages but in the New York City slums where, everything being equal, it would actually be occurring.

Most of this opening, and many of the other best parts, were the work of Jerome Robbins. The driven and demanding genius of a choreographer had directed the show on Broadway and here staged the dances and shared the director's chair with Hollywood pro Robert Wise. The virtues of Robbins's meticulous take-after-take approach are self-evident; unfortunately, such work was so expensive that the original budget was entirely spent by the time the company moved from the New York locations back to Hollywood. Blaming Robbins for the overrun, the producers promptly fired him. He had already worked out the staging for the remaining musical numbers, which Wise finished on his own. The two men would eventually be awarded Oscars for their directing, while Robbins won a second, special statuette for his choreography. Impressed by neither the film industry nor the Academy Awards, he kept both trophies in his basement.

Top Rita Moreno, George Chakiris, Natalie Wood | **Bottom** Russ Tamblyn and the Jets

The Jets

At the time of its opening, one respected critic called *West Side Story* "the best film musical ever made," and many thought that it represented something of a new maturity for a kind of film often dismissed as "only entertainment." For certain, its greatest moments, such as the prologue, "America," and "The Rumble," are at the summit of musicals' achievements. Robbins's choreography fully warrants its landmark status, especially when danced by George Chakiris and the other gang members, and Rita Moreno is a complete knockout as Anita. It might be noted that, in hindsight, there are some touches of Hollywood gloss that peek through occasionally, and an over-reliance on dubbed voices. In a film as ambitious and finely wrought as this one, such compromises were probably deemed unavoidable.

The overall accomplishment will always be what matters the most, and in this case a great and difficult show was put onto film with an extraordinary amount of commitment by artists working at the peak of their powers. Few other films, musical or not, can boast of this great a distinction.

USS-138(R-33-5)

George Chakiris and co-director/choreographer Jerome Robbins on the set

Movie folklore holds that the Manhattan locations where the street scenes were shot were demolished to make way for Lincoln Center. Almost, but not quite. The massive renewal project that created Lincoln Center was indeed underway in 1960, when filming occurred, but the actual street where the action was staged was a few blocks north, on a block that no longer exists. It used to be West 68th Street, between West End and Amsterdam Avenues, and is now the site of Lincoln Towers.

• • •

George Chakiris, who had played Bernardo in the London production of *West Side Story*, was greeted in 1961 as an exciting newcomer, which was half right. Audiences who did not know his name had already seen him dancing in a dozen 1950s musicals, including *Gentlemen Prefer Blondes*, where he's alongside Marilyn Monroe in "Diamonds Are a Girl's Best Friend."

Natalie Wood and Richard Beymer

MUSICALLY SPEAKING

As with Leslie Caron in *Gigi*, Natalie Wood was crushed when she learned that her vocals of Maria's songs would be dubbed by Marni Nixon. In a later time, Wood's sweet if underpowered singing voice would probably have been enhanced and allowed to stand. A similar fate befell one of Wood's costars, Russ Tamblyn, when his own "Jet Song" was replaced by that of Tucker Smith, who plays Ice onscreen. Tamblyn's version, it should be noted, is really quite good.

MORE TO SEE

Gypsy (1962): Natalie Wood sings in her own voice, in a controversial movie adaptation

Bye Bye Birdie (1963): Dancing teens of a different kind

Richard Beymer, George Chakiris, Russ Tamblyn

THE MUSIC MAN

WARNER BROS., 1962 | COLOR (TECHNICOLOR)/TECHNIRAMA, 151 MINUTES

DIRECTOR AND PRODUCER: MORTON DACOSTA   SCREENPLAY: MARION HARGROVE, BASED ON THE MUSICAL PLAY BY MEREDITH WILLSON AND FRANKLIN LACEY   SONGS: MEREDITH WILLSON   CHOREOGRAPHER: ONNA WHITE   STARRING: ROBERT PRESTON (HAROLD HILL), SHIRLEY JONES (MARIAN PAROO), BUDDY HACKETT (MARCELLUS WASHBURN), HERMIONE GINGOLD (EULALIE MACKECHNIE SHINN), PAUL FORD (MAYOR GEORGE SHINN), PERT KELTON (MRS. PAROO), THE BUFFALO BILLS (SCHOOL BOARD), TIMMY EVERETT (TOMMY DJILAS), SUSAN LUCKEY (ZANEETA SHINN), RONNY [RON] HOWARD (WINTHROP PAROO)

In the early 1900s, a phony "professor of music" sets out to swindle the citizens of a small Iowa town.

The Music Man could have gone wrong in any number of ways, and happily it didn't. The high-energy Broadway hit comes through just fine on film, including and especially its explosive, magnetic star, Robert Preston.

In the Broadway of 1957, Meredith Willson's tale of a charismatic conman and his musical reformation seemed to come out of virtually nowhere. Based in part on Willson's early-life experience in Mason City, Iowa, the show's predictable corniness was far overshadowed by its exuberance, heart, and musicality. (That talk-in-train-rhythm opening scene is still a knockout.) There was also inventive choreography by Onna White and, most especially, the boundlessly energetic and altogether irresistible Preston, as "Professor" Harold Hill. For two decades a reliable second-rank actor in film and sometimes theater, Preston was as unexpected as the show itself, winning a Tony Award and owning the role as much as Yul Brynner held the copyright on the King of Siam. With all this, Preston wasn't a sure thing for the movie. Jack L. Warner was seldom averse to the notion of replacing a stage player with a movie name, and he considered bypassing Preston in favor of Frank Sinatra or Cary Grant. Grant allegedly responded by saying that he not only refused to

be in the film, but if Preston didn't play Hill, he would not see it, either. The barbershop quartet known as the Buffalo Bills also made the transfer, as did Onna White and the original director, Morton DaCosta. DaCosta's first film, *Auntie Mame*, was a huge hit that frequently betrayed its stage origins. He would work in a much more cinematic mode on *The Music Man*, whose two and a half hours go by very fast.

Preston is as much a marvel here as he had been on Broadway, and one of the happiest aspects of his performance is that it's exactly the right size. Too many theater performers

"Marian the Librarian": Shirley Jones

overshoot the scale when they're called on to play to a camera, or else someone does a role hundreds of times onstage and, by the time of the movie, is either stale or bored. Preston's long film experience ensures that none of those things happen. Dynamic patter and theatrical gestures are all part of Hill's scam, and when real feeling is needed and the camera comes closer, Preston can scale down. While all the players are good, the one who perhaps best equals him is the remarkable eight-year-old Ronny Howard. He'd already been playing Opie Taylor for two seasons on *The Andy Griffith Show*, and his Winthrop is sweet, genuine, and, in "Gary, Indiana," joyously alive. There are also such delights as Pert Kelton, repeating her Broadway role, and the formidable Hermione Gingold, as Mayor Shinn's aggressively affected wife. As usual, she is magnificently baroque, and who would have it any other way?

Had it hit the movies a couple of years earlier, *The Music Man* would likely have been diluted, cut down, and coarsened. A few years later, lost in the flood of Broadway adaptations, it would have been overproduced and stodgy. Another decade and it might have seemed hopelessly dated. How fortunate, then, that it happened at just the right moment. The show deserves that much care and respect, and so, always, will Mr. Preston.

WHAT'S MORE

Barbara Cook, the show's Tony-winning Marian the Librarian, tested to play the role on film but was passed over in favor of Shirley Jones, an Oscar-winner and movie musical veteran. Cook—who never did appear in movies—commented in her autobiography that while she enjoyed Jones's performance, the film's depiction of River City seemed too pristine and clean-scrubbed. She underscored her assessment by adding, "Put bluntly, the horses never shit in those streets."

• • •

When Shirley Jones learned during filming that she was pregnant, producer/director DaCosta asked her to keep it a secret. The cat got let out of the bag, as it were, when she and Preston were doing the love scene on the bridge and her unborn child raised such a ruckus that even Preston could feel the kick. Many years later, the now-grown-up Patrick Cassidy introduced himself to Robert Preston, who responded with, "We've already met."

Opposite "Seventy-Six Trombones": Robert Preston | **Right** Shirley Jones, Ronny Howard, Robert Preston

The closing scene of the band badly playing Beethoven is, with a short musical finale, the way the play ends; the huge "dream" spectacle seen here was a movie invention, and not everyone who loved the show was or is a fan. While it does seem a kind of Hollywood thing to do, the fact is that by the time of the movie, "Seventy-Six Trombones" had become an American march favorite on a level with Sousa. It was thought, most likely accurately, that audiences would expect it at the finale—and who wouldn't want to see that grandly rocking strut Preston does while it plays?

MORE TO SEE

The Unsinkable Molly Brown (1964): Meredith Willson's other Broadway hit, with Debbie Reynolds in her favorite role

Victor/Victoria (1982): Preston and Julie Andrews in first-rate form

"Till There Was You": Shirley Jones and Robert Preston

THE UMBRELLAS OF CHERBOURG (LES PARAPLUIES DE CHERBOURG)

PARC FILM/TWENTIETH CENTURY-FOX, 1964 | **COLOR** (EASTMANCOLOR), **91 MINUTES**

DIRECTOR AND SCREENPLAY: **JACQUES DEMY**   PRODUCER: **MAG BODARD**   MUSIC: **MICHEL LEGRAND**   STARRING: **CATHERINE DENEUVE (GENEVIÈVE EMERY), NINO CASTELNUOVO (GUY FOUCHER), ANNE VERNON (MADAME EMERY), MARC MICHEL (ROLAND CASSARD), ELLEN FARNER (MADELEINE), MIREILLE PERREY (TANTE ÉLISE), JEAN CHAMPION (AUBIN), PIERRE CADEN (BERNARD), JEAN-PIERRE DORAT (JEAN)**   SINGING VOICES: **DANIELLE LICARI (GENEVIÈVE), JOSÉ BARTEL (GUY), CHRISTIANE LEGRAND (MADAME EMERY), GEORGES BLANESS (ROLAND), CLAUDINE MEUNIER (MADELEINE), CLAIRE LECLERC (TANTE ÉLISE)**

After her boyfriend is drafted to fight in the Algerian war, a young woman discovers she is pregnant.

A deliriously romantic swirl of song and color and heartbreak, Jacques Demy's lyrical love story is a film and musical like no other. The director's intention could not have been clearer: "I would like to make people cry."

Another goal was to make it musically seamless in a way that recalled early René Clair. Demy had termed his first film, *Lola*, "a musical without music," albeit with a score by Michel Legrand, and for *Umbrellas* he wrote a script

that Legrand would set completely to music, without spoken dialogue. Even for France, this was a daring (if not eccentric) concept, and it took a full year for Demy to find the financing. As Clair had done, he maintained exhaustive control over everything, including an extraordinarily forward color design and a soundtrack prerecorded by professional singers. The result was a sensation in Europe, America, and nearly everywhere else, garnering top prizes at the Cannes Festival and multiple Academy Award nominations. Two years later, Demy directed Deneuve in *The Young Girls of Rochefort*, another bright-hued, no-dialogue fantasia, to a more mixed response. Nor, despite further interesting work, would Demy reach such a pinnacle again.

It shouldn't work under any circumstances, this richly layered pastry of music, design, and heartache, and yet, for millions, it does. Why? The simple answer is that Demy, while courting and skirting self-indulgence at every turn, knew exactly how to pull it off. Perhaps the most apt word for the whole experience, in its music, color, and drama, is "saturation." Everything is piled on like there's no tomorrow, yet the excesses, when taken all together, balance each other out. From jazzy, hopeful beginning to icily sad finish, *Umbrellas* sustains its spell without seeming mechanical or overcalculated or, worse, insincere. For this, much credit must go to the prolific and gifted Legrand. He may be most recognized for the melodic gift so apparent in the big ballad known in the United States as "I Will Wait for You," but his skill also extends to making something musically interesting out of

Catherine Deneuve

even the simplest conversations between a girl and her mother, or a guy and his pals.

The cast, too, helps things along, with Deneuve and Castelnuovo looking both convincing and impossibly beautiful while mouthing all those musical lines. This was the role that made Deneuve a star, and not merely on account of her appearance. As for the auteur himself, Demy clearly revels in this self-contained world he's created, even in the face of such unwelcome intrusions as life, pregnancy, and the Algerian war. Those who succumb to his vision will swoon at the romance and may, by the end of it, accede to his intention and have a good cry. The experience is far more an immersion than a wallow, and small wonder that some enterprising later musicals bear the Demy stamp in one way or another. *La La Land* is especially noteworthy in this regard, not least because director Damien Chazelle has cited *Umbrellas* as his favorite film.

Obviously, this special and specialized film is not for all audiences, nor even for all musical aficionados. Its hypnotic allure has always made it a film apart, and those who adore it would not have things any other way.

Top to Bottom | Nino Castelnuovo and Catherine Deneuve | Catherine Deneuve and Nino Castelnuovo | Director Jacques Demy and Catherine Deneuve on the set

WHAT'S MORE

The hardest part for the actors came in coordinating their performances to a soundtrack that had already predetermined their delivery and much of their movement. Demy and Legrand decided that it would help them to actually sing along with the recording during filming, to deepen their connection to the music and produce convincing throat movements. Do it loud, Legrand advised them, and scream if necessary. They followed his directions dutifully, and the composer's opinion of how they sounded while doing so was quite to the point: "It was awful."

• • •

As if there wasn't enough sensory overload from the soundtrack, Demy also wanted a similar effect from the visuals. To that end, he worked with production designer Bernard Evein in much the same way that he did with Legrand, coordinating the colors as much as the musical lines. As any viewer of *Umbrellas* will attest, there are few movies where wallpaper plays a more prominent role, especially when its color or even its pattern matches a performer's costume. Demy's desire was to create, as he termed it "a singing Matisse," and it must be admitted that, in a very 1960s Pop Art sort of way, this is exactly what he did.

MUSICALLY SPEAKING

Although much of the music in *Umbrellas* would be categorized as sung speech instead of stand-alone songs, two moments of the score were successfully excerpted. Both were outfitted with English lyrics by Norman Gimbel, and "I Will Wait for You" was Oscar-nominated as Best Song. The second, bouncier Legrand tune had originally been written for Demy's *Lola* and found international popularity as "Watch What Happens." It was largely because of this pair, and *Umbrellas*, that Legrand became one of the busiest and most identifiable film composers of all time.

MORE TO SEE

The Young Girls of Rochefort (1967): Demy/Deneuve, plus Gene Kelly and George Chakiris

Dancer in the Dark (2000): Lars von Trier directs Deneuve and Björk.

Catherine Deneuve and Anne Vernon

A HARD DAY'S NIGHT

SHENSON/UNITED ARTISTS, 1964 | BLACK AND WHITE, 87 MINUTES

DIRECTOR: RICHARD LESTER   PRODUCER: WALTER SHENSON   SCREENPLAY: ALUN OWEN   SONGS: JOHN LENNON AND PAUL MCCARTNEY   STARRING: JOHN LENNON (JOHN), PAUL MCCARTNEY (PAUL), GEORGE HARRISON (GEORGE), RINGO STARR (RINGO), WILFRID BRAMBELL (GRANDFATHER), NORMAN ROSSINGTON (NORM), JOHN JUNKIN (SHAKE), VICTOR SPINETTI (TV DIRECTOR), ANNA QUAYLE (MILLIE)

A day in the life of the Beatles, with interference from Paul's grandfather.

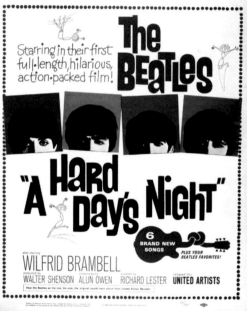

A *Hard Day's Night* is an everlasting delight, and not simply because it stars probably the most famous rock group of them all. It was, and is, the nature of pop phenomena that fame and idolatry hit fast, burn brightly, and peter out. Even in these, the Beatles were different: their music had far more craft and substance than usual, and their personalities and look were engaging without seeming affected. There were also the fans: endless millions of mainly young women screaming and swooning with an intensity that put earlier mobs to shame. Given the furor, it was inevitable that the Beatles would star in a film, just as Elvis had done and other singers would do throughout the entire history of sound film. Far less predictable was the fact that their movie was a work of wit and joy.

Depicting a slightly fanciful version of the real quartet, *A Hard Day's Night* takes an amused look at sudden celebrity and its impact on four nice, if occasionally bewildered, young men from Liverpool. Paul is reasonably self-aware, George lives on his own island, Ringo has a chip on his shoulder, and John is something of a benevolent, impudent madman. Together and sometimes separately, they must cope with cosmic fame, near-rabid fans, unreasonable professional demands, and Paul's appallingly mischief-prone

Top The Beatles in the coming-attractions trailer
Bottom Paul McCartney, George Harrison, Ringo Starr, John Lennon

grandfather. Their inherently good natures always see them through, at least enough to keep them grounded and able to perform some truly wonderful songs written by John and Paul.

The Fab Four would have read well on film under nearly any circumstances, but it is director Richard Lester who turns them into cinematic conquerors. Working with the same low budget as other rock movies, Lester made a virtue of the imposed limitations by bringing imagination and energy to the fore, using the songs as background scoring and in performance, without bogus integration. The music, as depicted here, is what keeps the quartet grounded, along with their senses of humor and of the absurd. Only on rare occasions are they allowed to escape the chaos and screaming, as in their playground romp to "Can't Buy Me Love." Here, especially, is where Lester cuts loose as much as the Beatles, with the same manic editing that, in less than two decades, would form a cornerstone for the new realm of music video. This is one of many repercussions *A Hard Day's Night* would have on film and rock music. It looked ahead to the

documentaries of later years, even "mockumentaries" like *This Is Spinal Tap*, and to new ways to promote and market musicians.

Most importantly, it showed that, where pop music was concerned, film could be far more than simply an ancillary prop. Seldom did its emulators come close to the original, not even when the Beatles reteamed with Lester a year later for a follow-up. In *Help!*, the frenzy of the fans is replaced by a great deal of running around, and the near-documentary feeling has morphed into brightly colored nonsense. (Still, however, with really good songs.) Only the later animated *Yellow Submarine* and the documentary *Let It Be* lay ahead, on film, before the Beatles disbanded. And what a legacy.

When *A Hard Day's Night* was being initially planned, someone probably had the notion that a Beatles film could be done fast and cheaply, make some money, and be fast forgotten. No one, it's safe to say, envisioned that it would be a groundbreaker, let alone a classic movie musical. The Beatles broke all kinds of rules, didn't they?

WHAT'S MORE

The near-poverty-level budget for this film was a sure indicator of how little United Artists believed in it. The company was, in fact, far less interested in producing a movie than in releasing a soundtrack album, to be issued on United Artists Records instead of the group's usual label, EMI/Capitol. Few involved would have predicted that in its first week of play in the United States, in a time long before make-or-break opening weekends, *A Hard Day's Night* grossed something like sixteen times its original cost.

• • •

If the film's off-the-wall brilliance was a surprise to everyone, there was some advance notice that this was an unconventional project. The coming-attractions trailer, shown in many theaters, interspersed clips from the film—mostly of screaming fans—with a scene of the Beatles discussing the film while comfortably seated in a pair of baby carriages. Imagine Elvis, or anyone else, doing such a thing.

MUSICALLY SPEAKING

The concert near the end is both a valuable record of the early-prime Beatles style and an accurate depiction of how their audiences behaved. It was shot in London's now-demolished Scala Theatre on March 31, 1964, with, as is quite apparent, a live audience. ("You Can't Do That," filmed as part of the set, was cut at the last minute. The footage survives.) Among the male minority in the crowd is a future star: the thirteen-year-old Phil Collins can be spotted if you know where to look. It took little direction to get the audience to yell uncontrollably and cry hysterically; they were at a Beatles concert, and such things came naturally.

MORE TO SEE

Yellow Submarine (1968): The Beatles, psychedelically animated

The Last Waltz (1978): Another group, The Band, and another major director, Martin Scorsese

Opposite Paul McCartney and Wilfrid Brambell
Right Ringo Starr, John Lennon, George Harrison, director Richard Lester, Paul McCartney on the set

MARY POPPINS

BUENA VISTA, 1964 | COLOR (TECHNICOLOR), 139 MINUTES

DIRECTOR: ROBERT STEVENSON PRODUCER: WALT DISNEY SCREENPLAY: BILL WALSH AND DON DAGRADI, BASED ON THE STORIES BY P. L. TRAVERS SONGS: RICHARD M. SHERMAN AND ROBERT B. SHERMAN CHOREOGRAPHERS: MARC BREAUX AND DEE DEE WOOD STARRING: JULIE ANDREWS (MARY POPPINS), DICK VAN DYKE (BERT/MR. DAWES SR.), DAVID TOMLINSON (GEORGE BANKS), GLYNIS JOHNS (WINIFRED BANKS), KAREN DOTRICE (JANE BANKS), MATTHEW GARBER (MICHAEL BANKS), ED WYNN (UNCLE ALBERT), HERMIONE BADDELEY AND RETA SHAW (DOMESTICS), ELSA LANCHESTER (KATIE NANNA), JANE DARWELL (THE BIRD WOMAN)

A nanny with unusual talents helps bring a London family closer together.

There's magic here, and if you saw it as a child, you've never forgotten it, or forgotten her. This wondrous combination of talent and technique is a dazzling introduction to a new star, and one of the best original musicals ever made.

Long before the words "brand" and "franchise" came into (over)use when discussing films, *Mary Poppins* cut to the essence of everything good bearing the name Walt Disney. Disney had been finding ways to set film to music since *Steamboat Willie*, in 1928, and *Mary Poppins* was the happy culmination of both his love affair with music and his drive to make live-action movies that were as special as his cartoons. He had long wanted to film the P. L. Travers stories of the magical, no-nonsense nanny, but Travers herself was leery of what might happen if her Poppins got the Disney treatment. (She finally said yes and, true to form, later regretted that she had.) Meanwhile, in 1961, the studio had a go at its first live-action musical fantasy, and the best thing about *Babes in Toyland* was that it taught everyone at Disney what not to do. In casting, writing, design, musical presentation, special effects, and sheer panache, *Mary Poppins* corrected all the mistakes *Toyland* had made. It also quickly became the highest-earning Disney film up to that time.

A movie as involved and busy as this could have gone hopelessly awry: a shaky or cloying tone, unsuitable songs, an overdose of special effects, too much Disney icing atop an insufficient cake. In avoiding those pitfalls, it manages to soar. For that, great credit must go to three names, one Andrews and two Shermans. Since she had been denied the chance to make her film debut in *My Fair Lady*, *Poppins* became, for Julie Andrews, the greatest consolation prize in film history. (That truly deserved Best Actress Oscar didn't hurt, either.) Without hitting any sort of wrong note, Andrews dominates and triumphs on film precisely as Poppins does in the Banks home: through sensibly and generously knowing exactly what she's doing at all times. When she's in charge, none of it—the penguin waiters

"Step in Time": Dick Van Dyke

or tea parties on the ceiling or prancing chimney sweeps—seems either superfluous or impossible, and everyone in front of and behind the camera seems inspired. This becomes especially true with the words and music of the Sherman brothers, which suit the characters and situations effortlessly. Propelling the story with ease, they are also able to take the time for such marvelous detours as "Supercalifragilisticexpialidocious." Would the songs seem the same, or sound so right, without Andrews? Hardly. Her clear tone and warm phrasing makes them seem, as Mary would say, practically perfect, and the tender of heart can be alerted that they may wipe away one small tear during "Feed the Birds."

It goes without saying that after this, there were further attempts at family-style musicals at Disney and elsewhere. The likes of *Doctor Dolittle* (1967), *Chitty Chitty Bang Bang* (1968), *Willy Wonka and the Chocolate Factory* (1971), *Bedknobs and Broomsticks* (1971), and others all owed their existence to *Poppins*. So did the inevitable stage version of *Poppins* that Disney produced forty years after the movie opened. Even so, *Mary Poppins* is a once-in-a-lifetime film, and Julie Andrews is an equally rare talent. They belong together.

"Jolly Holiday": Dick Van Dyke and Julie Andrews

Top Dick Van Dyke and Julie Andrews
Bottom "Let's Go Fly a Kite": Karen Dotrice, Glynis Johns, Matthew Garber, David Tomlinson

WHAT'S MORE

Everyone in Hollywood knew that the head of Warner Bros. had kept Julie Andrews out of the film of *My Fair Lady*. When she won a Golden Globe award for playing Mary Poppins, Andrews exacted an especially classy revenge. To end her gracious acceptance speech, she thanked "the man who made all this possible in the first place, Jack L. Warner." There were gasps from the audience, and then applause and loud cheers. Even from Warner himself.

• • •

Mary Poppins is one of the few films to spawn a "behind the scenes" movie that is not a documentary. *Saving Mr. Banks* (2013) told the story of Disney's ultimately successful attempt to convince P. L. Travers that he could film her stories, with Emma Thompson playing Travers and Tom Hanks as Disney. Somewhat softened and glamorized in the great Disney tradition, it was also reasonably convincing and extremely entertaining.

MUSICALLY SPEAKING

In its music, lyrics, and mix of animation and live action, "Jolly Holiday" is one of the best numbers in the film. The voices behind those cartoon characters include Marni Nixon, who gave Eliza Doolittle her voice after Julie Andrews was denied the role, and the longtime character actor J. Pat O'Malley. O'Malley also coached Dick Van Dyke in his Cockney accent, which was well and good except that O'Malley's background was more Irish than British and he had little experience with Cockney. Hence the one unconvincing part of an otherwise excellent performance.

> ### MORE TO SEE
>
> *Willy Wonka and the Chocolate Factory* (1971): The original, and still good
>
> *Frozen* (2013): That Disney brand still works

Left Dick Van Dyke, Julie Andrews, Matthew Garber, Karen Dotrice
Right "A Spoonful of Sugar": Julie Andrews

MY FAIR LADY

WARNER BROS., 1964 | COLOR (TECHNICOLOR)/SUPER PANAVISION 70, 170 MINUTES

DIRECTOR: **GEORGE CUKOR**   PRODUCER: **JACK L. WARNER**   SCREENPLAY: **ALAN JAY LERNER, BASED ON HIS MUSICAL PLAY,** **FROM THE PLAY** *PYGMALION* **BY GEORGE BERNARD SHAW**   SONGS: **FREDERICK LOEWE (MUSIC) AND ALAN JAY LERNER (LYRICS)**   CHOREOGRAPHER: **HERMES PAN**   STARRING: **AUDREY HEPBURN (ELIZA DOOLITTLE), REX HARRISON (PROFESSOR HENRY HIGGINS), STANLEY HOLLOWAY (ALFRED P. DOOLITTLE), WILFRID HYDE-WHITE (COLONEL PICKERING), GLADYS COOPER (MRS. HIGGINS), JEREMY BRETT (FREDDY EYNSFORD-HILL), THEODORE BIKEL (ZOLTAN KARPATHY), MONA WASHBOURNE (MRS. PEARCE), ISOBEL ELSOM (MRS. EYNSFORD-HILL)**

A phonetics professor wagers that he can transform a Cockney flower seller into a lady.

The biggest Broadway musical up to 1964 became the costliest and most publicized movie musical. A glorious show, a dazzling production, a cartload of Oscars, and a little bit of controversy. Quite a package.

Anybody could have predicted that a film of *My Fair Lady* would be a hit. On Broadway, it was such a smash that there were jokes about how hard it was to get tickets, and it was a show many people deeply loved. With its dazzling score, and star performances, and spot-on adaptation of Shaw's *Pygmalion*, it was so effective that even the romanticized ending fit in well. In an age of high-ticket Broadway adaptations this was, by far, the biggest—so much so that almost no musical had ever cost the $5.5 million Jack L. Warner spent simply to acquire the film rights. When all was said and done it was, at $17 million, one of the two most expensive films yet made in the United States. (*The Greatest Story Ever Told* was the other.) The magnitude of these figures ensured that the filmmakers would play things safely, if grandly, and take as few chances as possible.

No one, it was concluded, could be Higgins other than Rex Harrison, and since he was not considered a major film star, the casting of the female lead became a major consideration. Call it "Who's Eliza?" or "Audrey versus Julie," it was the most fraught wrangle to hit film since Elizabeth Taylor's *Cleopatra* scandals. Julie Andrews, the definitive Eliza onstage, had never appeared in a feature film. By contrast, Audrey Hepburn was a huge movie name, if few people's first conception of a Cockney guttersnipe. In the end, Warner went with the bankable star, while Andrews played Mary Poppins. She won an Oscar while Hepburn was not nominated, and *My Fair Lady* was a big hit that made most people extremely happy.

It might be said, with both irreverence and respect, that the film of *My Fair Lady* could be considered something of a footnote after all the commotion with the money, casting, headlines, success, and awards. What can definitely be

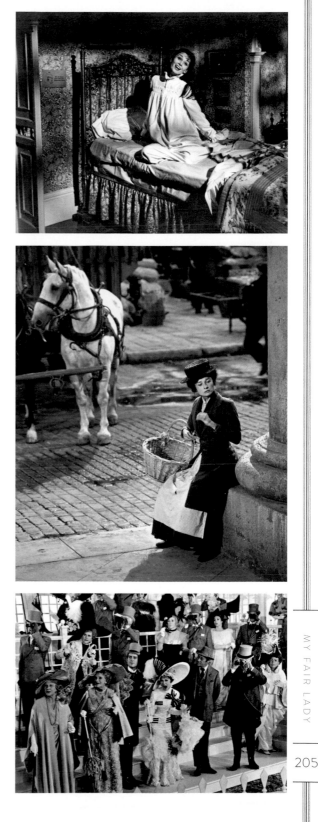

Top to Bottom   "I Could Have Danced All Night": Audrey Hepburn | Audrey Hepburn | Isobel Elsom, Gladys Cooper, Jeremy Brett, Audrey Hepburn, Rex Harrison, Wilfrid Hyde-White

noted is that, for many people, *My Fair Lady* stands at the pinnacle of shows put on film, with awe-inspiring detail and care going into loving re-creations of all its grand stage moments. Everything is pretty much where and as it should be. Audiences continue to thrill to the gorgeous soundtrack and swoon over the stunning production and that central romantic clash. Given all the circumstances, it was probably inevitable that the filmmakers would opt for a careful, painstaking approach to the material, and the reception given the film (in 1964 and later on) has certainly made this decision justifiable.

My Fair Lady is widely considered to be one of the greatest of all musicals, and the passion it engenders has sometimes prompted spirited discussion regarding its cinematic incarnation. In any case, it's an indisputable fact that, for millions, it remains one of the great movie musicals, eye-popping, truly loverly, and quite close to ideal.

WHAT'S MORE

George Cukor had directed literally dozens of classic movies before winning an Oscar for *My Fair Lady*. With *Little Women* (1933), *Dinner at Eight*, *Camille*, *Gaslight*, *Adam's Rib*, *Born Yesterday*, and the 1954 *A Star Is Born* as just a few of the items on his résumé, it's not unfair to say that his *Fair Lady* prize qualifies as a Lifetime Achievement Award.

• • •

Publicized as it was, the Audrey/Julie controversy would have been far more fraught had not the two ladies themselves been such, well, ladies. In fact, they became friends, and neither ever spoke disparagingly of the other. Eventually, Andrews later recalled, Hepburn admitted that she shouldn't have played Eliza. "Julie, you *should* have done the role," she said, "but I didn't have the guts to turn it down." Small comfort is comfort nevertheless.

Opposite Audrey Hepburn and Rex Harrison | **Above** Rex Harrison

"Ascot Gavotte"

MUSICALLY SPEAKING

The Ascot sequence is a highlight in *My Fair Lady*, and that marvelous Gavotte—sweet music and hilariously deadpan words—can't ever go wrong. As one would expect, it gets the full treatment here, with stylization and theatricality that are something of a contrast to the more literal tone taken elsewhere in the movie. Cecil Beaton's black-and-white designs are brilliant, and Hepburn's entrance is a genuine showstopper. The dress (and Hepburn) would have been stunning enough, but the audacity of that hat is simply breathtaking. So is the amount the ensemble fetched at a 2011 auction: including the premium, it was well over $4 million.

MORE TO SEE

Bells Are Ringing (1960): Judy Holliday in her Broadway hit, directed by Vincente Minnelli

How to Succeed in Business without Really Trying (1967): Yet another Broadway success, adapted with fidelity and skill

THE SOUND OF MUSIC

TWENTIETH CENTURY-FOX, 1965 | COLOR (DELUXE)/TODD-AO, 174 MINUTES

DIRECTOR AND PRODUCER: ROBERT WISE   SCREENPLAY: ERNEST LEHMAN, BASED ON THE MUSICAL PLAY BY HOWARD LINDSAY AND RUSSELL CROUSE, FROM *THE STORY OF THE TRAPP FAMILY SINGERS* BY MARIA VON TRAPP   SONGS: RICHARD RODGERS (MUSIC AND ADDITIONAL LYRICS) AND OSCAR HAMMERSTEIN II (LYRICS)   CHOREOGRAPHERS: MARC BREAUX AND DEE DEE WOOD   STARRING: JULIE ANDREWS (MARIA), CHRISTOPHER PLUMMER (CAPTAIN GEORG VON TRAPP), ELEANOR PARKER (THE BARONESS), RICHARD HAYDN (MAX DETWEILER), PEGGY WOOD (MOTHER ABBESS), CHARMIAN CARR (LIESL), HEATHER MENZIES (LOUISA), NICHOLAS HAMMOND (FRIEDRICH), DUANE CHASE (KURT), ANGELA CARTWRIGHT (BRIGITTA), DEBBIE TURNER (MARTA), KYM KARATH (GRETL)

In 1930s Austria, a postulant leaves her abbey to serve as governess to the children of a widowed naval officer.

"The Sound of Music": Julie Andrews

For a time, *The Sound of Music* was the most popular movie in history. It remains so loved, so internalized even, that many find it beyond criticism. It has been copied ruthlessly, yet continues to stand alone.

Surely, in 1965, *The Sound of Music* was the film that much of the world wanted, and it was hardly a coincidence that it was a musical. In reaction to the darker and more troubling currents of '60s life and filmmaking, its message of good deeds, faith, and song allying to defeat evil was fundamentally upbeat and reassuring. For many, going to see it was an event to be repeated

Top "Do Re Mi": Angela Cartwright, Charmian Carr, Nicholas Hammond, Julie Andrews, Duane Chase, Heather Menzies, Debbie Turner | **Bottom** Charmian Carr, Nicholas Hammond, Heather Menzies, Duane Chase, Angela Cartwright, Debbie Turner, Kym Karath, Christopher Plummer

numerous times, and for some the number of viewings went into double and even triple digits. If the sheer magnitude of its success came as a surprise to some, the unavoidable truth is that *The Sound of Music* has been and remains special and important to many, many people.

As extraordinarily well-made as it is, this film is unthinkable without Julie Andrews. From that ecstatic spin at the beginning all the way to the hope of a final mountain being climbed, she dominates every frame. Not even Mary Martin, in the original show, was the force and presence that Andrews is here. She had just showed the world, in *Mary Poppins*, that she knew how to take care of children and, like Poppins, Maria mixes common sense with wonder. Then there is the voice, so radiant and welcoming that it would take a really sour Von Trapp to not want to sing along with her.

Although Christopher Plummer is billed alongside Andrews, her true costars are Austria and Robert Wise. Make that "Austria as filmed by Robert Wise," with some of the most spectacular location shooting this side of *Lawrence of Arabia*. In contrast to musicals that seem hermetic and studio-bound, an audience at this one can all but breathe the fresh air. Every step of the way, from the convent to the Von Trapp estate to escaping the Nazis, Wise charts the course of Andrews and her cohorts with a professionalism that few musicals can equal. The Rodgers and Hammerstein songs, the kids, the puppets, the silken villainy of Eleanor Parker as the Baroness, the nuns, even the curtains made into clothes—all have a place in this staggeringly

well-executed production. Nothing is attempted that does not succeed, with every effect and moment crafted for maximum impact. Imagine how unbearably cloying it might have been in less confident hands, how pious and relentless. Instead, it's all been assembled with such skill that audiences continue to capitulate blissfully, just as they have for over half a century.

If judged by a court of its peers, *The Sound of Music* might not be voted "The Greatest Musical Ever Made." There's too much brilliant competition for that slot, after all. Here, then, is a big "However": for more people than possibly any other movie, it's this one—not the play, not the live TV version but this film—that defines what musicals are, and what they can give an audience. The devotion it has inspired is without parallel, and Lord knows this is one problem that doesn't need solving.

Julie Andrews and Peggy Wood

WHAT'S MORE

In its first release, *The Sound of Music* was the first film to go over the $100 million mark for its world gross. Its success pulled Twentieth Century-Fox out of its post-*Cleopatra* doldrums (although the profits were then lost on *Doctor Dolittle*, *Star!*, and *Hello, Dolly!*). Adjusted for inflation, *The Sound of Music* remains one of the most profitable films of all time, and *the* most successful musical, ever. When it became known inside the industry as *The Sound of Money*, no one meant it disrespectfully.

• • •

Between the glories of its Austrian scenery and the rabid devotion the film inspired, it was inevitable that there would be *Sound of Music*–inspired tours of Salzburg and its environs. These actually started as early as 1965 but took off in earnest in the 1970s. Visitors can sometimes be nonplussed to find how many of the locales, following standard movie practice, had been quite reconfigured for film. Without the tour, a casual viewer might never know, for example, that the front and rear of the Von Trapp estate were actually two completely separate places.

MUSICALLY SPEAKING

"Do-Re-Mi" is one of this film's undoubted highlights, both for the song's catchy simplicity and for its exuberant, wide-ranging staging. Plus, naturally, the way Andrews and the children perform it. All praise, then, to Marc Breaux and Dee Dee Wood, who scoured the Salzburg region in search of the locations, and to editor William Reynolds, whose work in this sequence alone likely earned him his Academy Award.

MORE TO SEE

Maytime (1937): Awesome professionalism from an earlier time, with Jeanette MacDonald and Nelson Eddy

Thoroughly Modern Millie (1967): Ms. Andrews, again, in good company and in great form

Top Angela Cartwright, Duane Chase, Debbie Turner, Julie Andrews, Nicholas Hammond, Kym Karath, Heather Menzies, Charmian Carr | **Left** Julie Andrews, Debbie Turner, Angela Cartwright, Heather Menzies, Christopher Plummer, Kym Karath, Nicholas Hammond, Charmian Carr, Eleanor Parker

FUNNY GIRL

COLUMBIA, 1968 | COLOR (TECHNICOLOR)/PANAVISION, 155 MINUTES

DIRECTOR: WILLIAM WYLER   PRODUCER: RAY STARK   SCREENPLAY: ISOBEL LENNART, BASED ON HER MUSICAL PLAY   SONGS: JULE STYNE (MUSIC) AND BOB MERRILL (LYRICS)   DIRECTOR, MUSICAL NUMBERS: HERBERT ROSS   STARRING: BARBRA STREISAND (FANNY BRICE), OMAR SHARIF (NICK ARNSTEIN), KAY MEDFORD (ROSE BRICE), ANNE FRANCIS (GEORGIA JAMES), WALTER PIDGEON (FLORENZ ZIEGFELD), LEE ALLEN (EDDIE RYAN), MAE QUESTEL (MRS. STRAKOSH), GERALD MOHR (BRANCA), FRANK FAYLEN (KEENEY), MITTIE LAWRENCE (EMMA)

Fanny Brice wins stardom in the *Ziegfeld Follies* and heartache when she falls in love with a gambler.

When a major star makes a sensational film debut, the earth shakes and the planets realign. Such things occur so rarely as to be legendary—which is as good a word as any to describe Barbra Streisand's arrival onto film in *Funny Girl*. She was hardly an unknown quantity. Few were unaware of the precociously talented young woman from Brooklyn with distinctive looks and an unforgettable way with a song. She had already conquered the recording industry, the stage, and television, and it stood to reason that a film career was at least a strong possibility.

It surprised virtually no one when her movie debut came in the film of her defining Broadway

Above "I'd Rather Be Blue": Barbra Streisand | **Right** "My Man": Barbra Streisand

hit, *Funny Girl*. Purportedly a biography of the singer and comedian Fanny Brice, it became even more of a one-woman show on film than on the stage, with Streisand appearing in nearly every scene and singing nearly every song. At a time when roadshow musicals were beginning their decline, *Funny Girl* ran and ran, with Streisand fans as impassioned a group of repeat viewers as those who loved *The Sound of Music*. Her triumph was nearly unconditional, and her Academy Award (shared with Katharine Hepburn) all but inevitable.

Although focused tightly on Fanny Brice's career and personal life, *Funny Girl* is lavish and at times spectacular, as crafted by a prestigious group of filmmakers. Foremost among these were producer Ray Stark, Brice's son-in-law, and director William Wyler, whose résumé encompassed multiple Oscars and more classics than nearly any other director could boast. Never before had he directed a musical, and his work on *Funny Girl* is conventional, professional, and fully aware that a major new star will always benefit from just the right kind of attentive presentation. A gilt-edged production, a somewhat deferential supporting cast, and lots and lots of lovingly photographed Barbra:

it was what people wanted and hoped for, and no one went away disappointed. Clowning in roller skates or toe shoes, wisecracking and romancing, singing her signature ballad "People," defying her tears in that "My Man" finale—she gives a virtuoso display as is seldom known, even possible, on film. The closest equivalent is probably Judy Garland in *A Star Is Born*, with its not-entirely-dissimilar plot arc. Still, the differences are many, especially as regards Garland's vulnerable outreach versus Streisand's all-conquering invincibility. If some prefer one to the other, both are valid ways to deploy immense talent. A more invidious comparison might come with their leading men. Where James Mason is heartbreaking, Omar Sharif is constricted by a one-dimensional role that compels Streisand to work all the harder to move things along to that teary conclusion. Since both Garland and Streisand have their deserved legions of fans and fanatics, it is the moviegoer's good fortune that these two big showcases exist to present their gifts so generously.

There would be many more successes for Streisand, on film as elsewhere, but comparatively few musicals. (One of them would be *Funny Girl*'s less-successful sequel, *Funny Lady*.) As an actor, director, and singer, she has endured as few others could. With all her achievements, *Funny Girl* remains special in a way not possible outside the premises of a big and well-crafted movie musical. No wonder Streisand-lovers hold it in such high esteem. And, truly, not just them.

"His Love Makes Me Beautiful":
Barbra Streisand

WHAT'S MORE

Streisand was considered such a sure thing that she was signed for her second movie, *Hello, Dolly!*, long before audiences had seen her in so much as one frame of film. This confidence was fiscal as well as artistic, given that *Dolly*'s astronomical $25 million cost was nearly twice that of *Funny Girl*. The fact that *Dolly* did nowhere near the business of its predecessor helped speed the end of musical blockbusters, and Streisand's participation in them.

• • •

Although only twenty-five when *Funny Girl* was shot, Streisand was already known as a meticulous perfectionist. Rumors were soon emanating from the set that she, not the esteemed Wyler, was in charge and calling the shots. They both denied the reports and stayed friends, yet the story persists that a Wyler colleague commiserated by telling him, "Give her a break—it's the first movie she's ever directed."

MUSICALLY SPEAKING

For many, the highlight of *Funny Girl* is "Don't Rain on My Parade," with its triumphant helicopter shot of Streisand and the Statue of Liberty, both with arms lifted. Herbert Ross conceived the number and, over two weeks, filmed it at multiple locations, including the Central Railroad Station in Jersey City; the U.S. Army's railroad track near Dover, New Jersey; the Brooklyn Navy Yard; and finally New York Harbor. Not since *The Great Ziegfeld*, and "A Pretty Girl Is Like a Melody," had a musical gone from its first half to intermission in so spectacular a fashion. The only downside came later when, in *Funny Lady*, Ross and Streisand attempted a weak copy ("Let's Hear It for Me") using an airplane instead of a tugboat. That one, fortunately, has passed from memory while "Parade" is as impressive and cinematic as ever.

> ### MORE TO SEE
>
> *The Rose* (1979): Enter Bette Midler, in a different kind of one-woman show
>
> *Coal Miner's Daughter* (1980): A more authentic musical biopic, with an Oscar-winning Sissy Spacek as Loretta Lynn

Omar Sharif and Barbra Streisand

OLIVER!

ROMULUS/COLUMBIA, 1968 | COLOR (TECHNICOLOR)/PANAVISION, 153 MINUTES

DIRECTOR: **CAROL REED** PRODUCER: **JOHN WOOLF** SCREENPLAY: **VERNON HARRIS, BASED ON THE MUSICAL PLAY BY LIONEL BART, FROM THE NOVEL** *OLIVER TWIST* **BY CHARLES DICKENS** SONGS: **LIONEL BART** CHOREOGRAPHER: **ONNA WHITE** STARRING: **RON MOODY (FAGIN), OLIVER REED (BILL SIKES), SHANI WALLIS (NANCY), MARK LESTER (OLIVER TWIST), JACK WILD (THE ARTFUL DODGER), HARRY SECOMBE (BUMBLE), HUGH GRIFFITH (MAGISTRATE), JOSEPH O'CONOR (MR. BROWNLOW), PEGGY MOUNT (MRS. BUMBLE), LEONARD ROSSITER (SOWERBERRY)**

A young boy escapes from a London orphanage and falls in with a band of pickpockets and their leader.

Who could imagine the grim and hopeful tale of Dickens's *Oliver Twist* as a successful musical? First on the London stage, then on Broadway, and finally as an Oscar-winning movie? This near-miracle is the work of composer/writer/lyricist Lionel Bart, who saw the potential lurking in the story of the boy from the workhouse. Much praise also to director Carol Reed, who made the show into such an exuberant, affecting piece of cinema.

Like *My Fair Lady*, *Oliver!* transformed a much-loved work into a truly integrated show, based by Bart on the 1948 David Lean film of *Oliver Twist*. This meant that large portions of the lengthy novel are gone, yet its spirit and

Top Mark Lester and Jack Wild | **Bottom** Mark Lester and Harry Secombe

"As Long As He Needs Me": Shani Wallis

most riveting components remain. The songs, for their part, are both tightly connected to the story and grand on their own terms—"Food, Glorious Food," "Where Is Love?," "Consider Yourself," "As Long As He Needs Me," and the rest form a magical procession of hits to match the best of Rodgers and Hammerstein. In less astute hands, it might have been something on the order of "Scenes from Dickens with Selected Song Interludes"; instead, it's a cohesive narrative in which drama, song, and even dance are all vital and essential. If it has slightly sentimentalized the novel, it remains faithful in its fashion.

The choice of Carol Reed was well in line with the "Broadway blockbuster" mentality of the time, which held that a revered director with no experience with musicals might bestow a kind of pedigree on an expensive ($10 million) project. As it emerged, Reed's steady and experienced hand with drama (*The Third Man*, *The Fallen Idol*, *Odd Man Out*) was a major asset. An unusually long rehearsal period enabled him to draw an expressive performance out of eight-year-old

Mark Lester, while the actors who had already done the show on the stage were guided to scale down their characterizations for the camera. In particular, the broad inflections Ron Moody had used when he created the role of Fagin were made deeper and subtler, resulting in a performance so definitive that Moody continued playing the role for much of the rest of his life.

With choreographer Onna White working in as meticulous and time-consuming a fashion as Reed, *Oliver!* took nearly seven months to film. Even for a major production, this was a long shoot, and the effort and cash were well spent. Not too reverent, too stagey, or, blessedly, beholden to movie gimmickry, it is one of the most finely calibrated of stage adaptations. Neither music, melodrama, nor comedy is slighted, and the production is astonishing in its detail. A few may find the 1960s hair of Shani Wallis (an excellent Nancy) a bit distracting, but overall the period feeling and Dickensian atmosphere are strikingly evocative.

Good as it is, *Oliver!* was nearly the end of the line for the 1960s run of prestigious, high-budget musicals. Only one more (*Fiddler on the Roof*) would be truly successful; the number grows to two if we count *Cabaret*, a free adaptation which was not really a roadshow attraction. Then, in the 1970s and beyond, taste and filmmaking moved into other areas. The six Academy Awards given to *Oliver!* were both an indication of its great merit and, as it turned out, a particularly shiny way to mark the end of an era. By the time another musical (*Chicago*) won the Best Picture award, the movies and the world had changed immeasurably.

WHAT'S MORE

It was no coincidence that the director shared a surname with his Bill Sikes. Oliver Reed was Sir Carol Reed's nephew, but nepotism was not a factor in his casting. The younger Reed was already prominent in British film and television, and was pretty much as tough off the screen as he looked on it. Sikes's one song in the show, "My Name," was removed for the film and, given Reed's grim performance, this renders the character even less human and more distanced from the others.

• • •

State-of-the-art for a 1968 production, *Oliver!* also looked ahead to the technology of the future. In a movie first, technician Joe Dunton devised a way to place and operate a video camera atop the film camera, thus enabling the director to see an instant playback and saving considerable quantities of time, money, and aggravation.

MUSICALLY SPEAKING

The nine-minute "Who Will Buy?" sequence is both inventive and, in its spectacle, an old-fashioned piece of movie magic. The whole of London's Bloomsbury Square was reconstructed on the back lot of Shepperton Studios, the cast of dancers and actors numbered over four hundred, and it took weeks to rehearse and shoot. The only giveaway for all the time and effort comes with a close look at the shadows cast on the ground. They change length frequently, thus demonstrating that, like many big numbers, this one was shot in many takes at various times of the day.

MORE TO SEE

Scrooge (1970): More musical Dickens

Sweeney Todd: The Demon Barber of Fleet Street (2007): Reimagined, strikingly, from the Sondheim success

---

Shani Wallis, Oliver Reed, Ron Moody

FIDDLER ON THE ROOF

UNITED ARTISTS, 1971 | COLOR (TECHNICOLOR)/PANAVISION, 181 MINUTES

DIRECTOR AND PRODUCER: NORMAN JEWISON   SCREENPLAY: JOSEPH STEIN, BASED ON HIS MUSICAL PLAY, FROM THE WRITINGS OF SHOLOM ALEICHEM   SONGS: JERRY BOCK (MUSIC) AND SHELDON HARNICK (LYRICS)   CHOREOGRAPHER: TOM ABBOTT

STARRING: TOPOL (TEVYE), NORMA CRANE (GOLDE), LEONARD FREY (MOTEL), MOLLY PICON (YENTE), PAUL MANN (LAZAR WOLF), ROSALIND HARRIS (TZEITEL), MICHELE MARSH (HODEL), NEVA SMALL (CHAVA), [PAUL] MICHAEL GLASER (PERCHIK), RAY[MOND] LOVELOCK (FYEDKA)

In pre-revolution Russia, Tevye the milkman copes with poverty, marrying off his daughters, and growing anti-Jewish hostility.

It's always stood apart, just a little, from the others. Call it, perhaps, a necessity—a work that's been absorbed and internalized in ways other musicals can't achieve. It has the trappings of a traditional show but, emotionally and culturally, has come to signify things beyond the usual scope of entertainment. On film, as in the theater, *Fiddler on the Roof* is a work of survival, faith, resilience, defiance, humor, and, of course, tradition.

Although some of its backers feared it might be "too Jewish" for general audiences, *Fiddler* became an instant classic when it opened on Broadway in 1964 and went on to become the longest-running show up to that time. Inevitably, there were apprehensions when it came time to make the film version. Was it perhaps too powerful for movies, or, putting it crassly again, "too Jewish"? So many other shows had been flattened or coarsened, and this one deserved better. There was, then, an immense sigh of relief when the *Fiddler* movie opened. It was big where it needed to be without being blown out of proportion or glitzed-up, the score was intact (two deletions), the no-star cast was terrific, it looked magnificent, and the director knew what he was doing. The show had been treated with love and respect and, what's more, with vitality. From the impassioned strains of Isaac Stern's opening violin solo and the rhythmic editing of "Tradition," all the way to the regret and hope of its conclusion, this *Fiddler* soars both as adaptation and as cinema.

It always comes down to a series of choices, and in this case they ended up being, mostly, spot-on. The greatest controversy came in not having Zero Mostel re-create his Tony-winning Tevye. Mostel himself remained bitter about it (a few "Passover" jokes were made), yet a look at his film work makes the choice fathomable. In *The Producers*, he's as outsized as he is magnetic, with gestures and reactions that may simply have been too much for the more restrained tone decided upon by the filmmakers. While Haim

"Do You Love Me?": Topol and Norma Crane

Topol, the Israeli actor who had played Tevye in the London production, was hardly a shrinking violet either, he was unfamiliar to most movie audiences. Large in person and personality, by turns genial and passionate, he dominates the film without overwhelming the material, the only caveat being that even with makeup and gray streaks, he may seem too young (thirty-five) for the put-upon milkman with five daughters.

The choice of director, too, was off the beaten path. Jerome Robbins, who had staged and choreographed the original production, declined a possible replay of his firing from *West Side Story*. Legend holds that United Artists then turned to Norman Jewison because he was believed, mistakenly, to be Jewish. More pertinently, Jewison was both hot and versatile, with such hits as *The Thomas Crown Affair* and the Oscar-winning *In the Heat of the Night*. With the aid of some magnificent location shooting (then Yugoslavia, now Croatia) and the earth-toned cinematography of Oswald Morris, Jewison makes *Fiddler* both grand and intimate, a tale of a family, a small village, and, crucially, a way of life.

Singing ghosts, young lovers, matchmakers, dancing, upheaval, and God and "Sunrise, Sunset": *Fiddler* manages to cover a great deal of territory in three hours. The wonder is that it keeps everything so vibrant, entertaining, and touching. "L'chaim!," Tevye and his friends sing, "To life!" How fortunate for the audience that they're willing to share this life so generously.

"Matchmaker": Rosalind Harris, Neva Small, Michele Marsh

WHAT'S MORE

Before Topol was cast, several famous actors were considered for the role of Tevye or let it be known they were interested. Danny Kaye and even Anthony Quinn might seem plausible, but Orson Welles? Marlon Brando? Plus, yes, Frank Sinatra, whose agent called Norman Jewison in an unsuccessful attempt to set up an audition.

• • •

Norma Crane, who had been active in television and film since the early 1950s, was cast as Golde after Anne Bancroft rejected the role as being too subsidiary. Crane began work on the film knowing she had breast cancer, a secret she shared with the producers, Jewison, and Topol. She died at age forty-four, less than two years after *Fiddler* opened.

MUSICALLY SPEAKING

As choreographed by Tom Abbott, the exterior-shot musical numbers in *Fiddler* are among the best of that type in any film, *The Sound of Music* included. "Matchmaker" is a particular delight, not least because of the luminous Rosalind Harris. She had already played Tzeitel on Broadway as a replacement for Bette Midler, who in turn had replaced the original. In the late 1980s, for a touring production of *Fiddler*, Harris moved up to the role of Golde—opposite her one-time cinematic dad, Topol. Swiftly fly the years, indeed.

> ### MORE TO SEE
>
> *Yentl* (1983): Barbra Streisand's directorial debut has obvious *Fiddler* parallels
>
> *Hair* (1979): Another loving Broadway transfer

"To Life": Topol

"If I Were a Rich Man": Topol

CABARET

ABC/ALLIED ARTISTS, 1972 | COLOR (TECHNICOLOR), 124 MINUTES

DIRECTOR AND CHOREOGRAPHER: BOB FOSSE   PRODUCER: CY FEUER   SCREENPLAY: JAY PRESSON ALLEN, BASED ON THE SCRIPT OF THE MUSICAL PLAY BY JOE MASTEROFF, FROM THE PLAY *I AM A CAMERA* BY JOHN VAN DRUTEN, AND CHRISTOPHER ISHERWOOD'S NOVEL *THE BERLIN STORIES*   SONGS: JOHN KANDER (MUSIC) AND FRED EBB (LYRICS)   STARRING: LIZA MINNELLI (SALLY BOWLES), MICHAEL YORK (BRIAN ROBERTS), HELMUT GRIEM (MAXIMILIAN VON HEUNE), JOEL GREY (MASTER OF CEREMONIES), FRITZ WEPPER (FRITZ WENDEL), MARISA BERENSON (NATALIA LANDAUER), ELISABETH NEUMANN-VIERTEL (FRAULEIN SCHNEIDER), HELEN VITA (FRAULEIN KOST), SIGRID VON RICHTHOFEN (FRAULEIN MAYR), GERD VESPERMANN (BOBBY)

On the eve of the Nazi takeover, a Berlin cabaret is the setting for onstage razzmatazz and offstage complications.

Dynamic and insightful, via the dark magician Bob Fosse, and one of the most brilliant of all movie musicals.

On the stage, this adaptation of Christopher Isherwood's *Berlin Stories*, and the subsequent play *I Am a Camera*, was a mix of conventional theater and less representational "concept." The scenes in Berlin's seedy Kit Kat Club, as presided over by the sinister master of ceremonies, alternated with two love stories, both ultimately unhappy. For this thoroughly reimagined film, the "plot" songs were jettisoned along with one of the doomed romances. In Bob Fosse's first film as a director, *Sweet Charity*, some outstanding and even innovative moments were hampered by old-style studio compromises. For *Cabaret*, with Fosse now in absolute control, every single element was part of an overall mosaic that reduced the show to its essence. With one important exception, he staged the musical numbers at the cabaret, all commenting on the characters and, more broadly, on the growing menace of Nazism.

From Grey's insidious "Wilkommen" to Minnelli's defiant insistence that life is a cabaret, not one thing was out of place, wasted or extrinsic. This, coming after years of increasingly frivolous and out-of-touch musicals, was bracing, relevant, and unsettling. Its Nazis seemed far more real (and evil) than those in *The Sound of Music*, its exploration of bisexuality was all but unknown in mainstream film, and it dared to proffer cynicism instead of optimism. Pauline Kael was among the critics who hoped that, post-*Cabaret*, there might be more musicals this mature and resourceful. But no, at least not around this time, or by these artists. Except for the deeply personal *All That Jazz*, Fosse never directed another movie musical. Nor would Liza Minnelli ever again have a film triumph on this level; her one major subsequent musical, *New York, New York*, was brave and deeply flawed. Instead of leading to new paths for musicals, *Cabaret* became, for many, the last supremely great one for many years.

How often has a movie musical ever reflected its director's vision with such relentless virtuosity? Fosse's grasp of the material was so powerful and sure that many subsequent productions of the stage version have tried, in various ways, to copy some of his effects, sometimes by using some of the alternate Kander and Ebb songs added to the film. ("Maybe This Time" actually predated the show by two years.) Ultimately, neither Fosse's work, nor that of his extraordinary collaborators, could be reproduced. A musical had never looked or moved or been edited like this one and, despite Fosse's impact, has not done so subsequently.

With its virtuosic score, bold juxtapositions of comedy and horror, and crushingly candid sense of irony, *Cabaret* is a work to inspire the utmost respect. Lest that sound too reverential, be aware that it's also tremendously enjoyable. It is, after all, a musical, and it's one of the best.

"Mein Herr": Liza Minnelli

Top "Money, Money": Joel Grey and Liza Minnelli | **Bottom** "Willkommen": Joel Grey

WHAT'S MORE

Was she good casting, or not? The argument raged in 1972, and continues in some circles, that Liza Minnelli was too talented—at least, too good a singer—to play the self-dramatizing, deluded Sally Bowles. Christopher Isherwood himself thought so, and in many stage productions the role is taken by women who may have Minnelli's acting ability but not her musical gifts. Consider, then, that the medium of film, with its close-up immediacy, might not favor a Sally who merely scrapes by in those formidable Kander/Ebb songs. Also, it's not difficult to imagine that Sally might always find a way to sabotage her own best ambitions. At any rate, the notion of this particular *Cabaret* without Minnelli is not remotely inviting.

• • •

Cabaret still holds the record for the most Oscar wins—eight—of any film that failed to take home the top prize. (That went, in 1973, to *The Godfather*.) That has to qualify as more than simply a backhanded compliment, and it might be added that, with two such outstanding films in competition, the Academy voters were being handed quite a difficult choice.

MUSICALLY SPEAKING

In "Tomorrow Belongs to Me," the only number not shot in the Kit Kat Club, neither the Nazi youth on the screen, nor the tenor singing on the soundtrack, was credited. The singer is an American, Mark Lambert, and the on-screen performer is a Bavarian actor, Oliver Collignon. Although a few find Fosse's staging somewhat heavy-handed, it remains, for most viewers, a stunner.

> ### MORE TO SEE
>
> *All That Jazz* (1979): All that Fosse, in a musical tour of the director's psyche
>
> *Nashville* (1975): A vastly different panorama, via Robert Altman

Liza Minnelli and director Bob Fosse on the set

THE ROCKY HORROR PICTURE SHOW

TWENTIETH CENTURY-FOX, 1975 | COLOR (EASTMANCOLOR), 100 MINUTES

DIRECTOR: JIM SHARMAN   PRODUCER: MICHAEL WHITE   SCREENPLAY: JIM SHARMAN AND RICHARD O'BRIEN, BASED ON THE MUSICAL PLAY BY O'BRIEN   SONGS: RICHARD O'BRIEN   STARRING: TIM CURRY (DR. FRANK-N-FURTER), SUSAN SARANDON (JANET WEISS), BARRY BOSTWICK (BRAD MAJORS), RICHARD O'BRIEN (RIFF RAFF), PATRICIA QUINN (MAGENTA), LITTLE NELL [NELL CAMPBELL] (COLUMBIA), JONATHAN ADAMS (DR. EVERETT V. SCOTT), PETER HINWOOD (ROCKY HORROR), MEAT LOAF (EDDIE), CHARLES GRAY (THE CRIMINOLOGIST)

A newly engaged couple with car trouble takes refuge in the castle of one Dr. Frank-N-Furter . . .

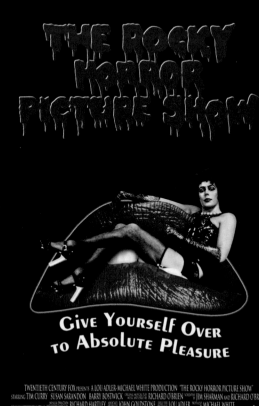

Within the cult that is *Rocky Horror*, the mainstream collides with the underground, the traditional with the insanely unconventional, the classic with the iconoclastic. Suffice it to say that in all musical film—make that all film, period—there's no phenomenon like this one.

It began, as so often, on the stage, with the amiably warped vision of writer-composer-actor Richard O'Brien, who conceived it as a combination horror spoof/comic book/

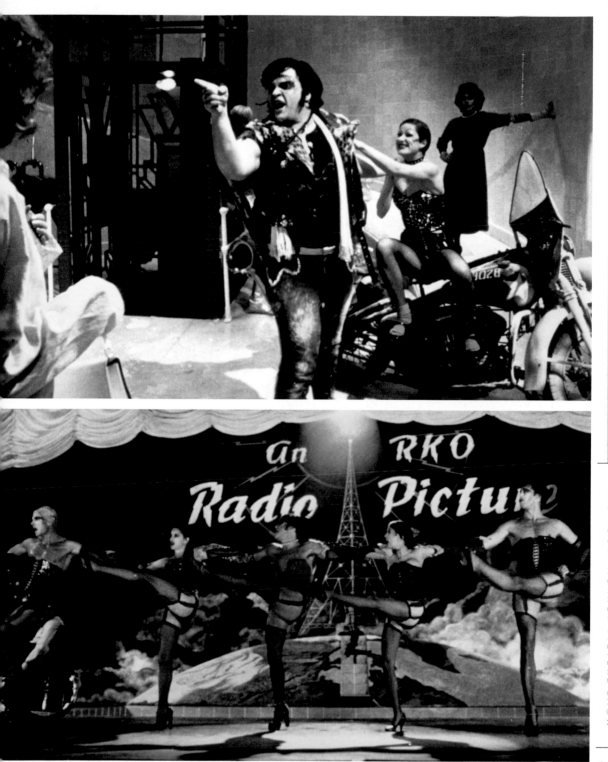

Top "Hot Patootie": Meat Loaf, Little Nell, Tim Curry | **Bottom** "Wild and Untamed Thing": Peter Hinwood, Little Nell, Tim Curry, Susan Sarandon, Barry Bostwick

rock-tinged fantasy. Directed by Jim Sharman, *The Rocky Horror Show* opened in London in 1973 and quickly created a furor. Within two years it had opened successfully in Los Angeles and unsuccessfully on Broadway, and had been filmed in the UK with a cast that (except for Susan Sarandon and Barry Bostwick) consisted almost entirely of veterans of the stage production.

Although its costs had been kept low, the film drew next to no business when it opened, and its reviews echoed that same enthusiasm. Then, like most flops, it skulked away and died, at least until midnight on April Fool's Day 1976, at the Waverly Theater in Manhattan's Greenwich Village. Midnight movies were, at that time, an increasingly popular way for off-beat and sometimes off-putting films like *Pink Flamingos* and *El Topo* to stimulate more devotion and chemical ingestion than they could in conventional screenings. It quickly became clear that *Rocky Horror* was a midnight cult movie far beyond others, with audiences, that, in effect, jumped into the movie. They talked and yelled back to the screen, came in costume and performed along with the on-screen actors, threw rice and did everything else short of creating a synthetic man or burning down the theater. The mania spread from one city to another and continues, at a less hysterical level, up to the present day—giving *Rocky Horror* the longest continual release of any film in history.

"Sweet Transvestite": Tim Curry

With its spoofing, gender-bending, and homage to Britain's Hammer horror movies, would *Rocky Horror* have had quite the same voracious effect had it not been a musical? No way, no less than with *Grease* or *The Wizard of Oz*. Music and dance are as essential to this film as they are to, say, *The Sound of Music*. They define the characters ("Sweet Transvestite"), set the tone ("Science Fiction/Double Feature"), and move the action forward ("I Can Make You a Man"), as in any conventional musical. Ultimately, in a song like "Don't Dream It," they celebrate this entire phantasmagoria of strangeness, parody, and weird acceptance. Whatever else *Rocky Horror* may mean to any viewer, it is inclusive, turning away no one and even welcoming the squares. Tim Curry's Dr. Frank-N-Furter takes sexual omniscience far beyond anything ever seen before on film, but he doesn't demand or need acceptance. Like everything and everyone else here, he's simply being his own unapologetic self, and singing and dancing while doing so.

Some viewers can only accept *Rocky Horror* within that frenzied context of audience participation that gave it such landmark status. Others prefer it straight, all other things being equal, without the water pistols and whatnot. Either way, and like other important or necessary musicals, it defies its naysayers, scoffs at its imitators (and that listless TV remake), invites in the newbies, blesses its faithful, and keeps on going. If movie musicals have often had the aura of a time warp, this is the one that takes it literally.

Top to Bottom | Tim Curry, Peter Hinwood, Susan Sarandon | Susan Sarandon and Barry Bostwick | "The Time Warp"

WHAT'S MORE

As fanatics are well aware, there are differences between the movie versions originally run in the UK and in midnight screenings in the United States. Brad and Janet's choruses of "Super Heroes" were deleted for the United States, the closing credits were redone with cast photos, and the reprise of "Science Fiction-Double Feature" replaced by "Time Warp." Essentially, it was felt that the American version needed to end on a slightly more upbeat note—which, given the level of audience enthusiasm, might not be totally necessary.

• • •

After the "*Rocky Horror* at Midnight" phenomenon began in earnest, circa 1977, a number of articles reported on and compared the frenzy in various cities. New Orleans often topped the list of most interactive audiences—justifiably, as this firsthand observer can testify. Besides some adept live performers down front who enacted the movie as it ran on the screen, there was the enterprising gentleman who, at Meat Loaf's entrance, rode a motorcycle down one aisle of the theater, across the stage, and back up the other aisle. Even with the smoke and exotic odors already in the auditorium, the gasoline smell managed to linger for quite some time.

MUSICALLY SPEAKING

In the original show, "Time Warp" came after "Sweet Transvestite." For the movie, Richard O'Brien decided that they should switch places, which has since become the accepted order for the now-slightly-reworked stage version. This change is logical, since after Frank makes his entrance and sings the show-stopping "Transvestite," even something as up-tempo as "Time Warp" might seem anticlimactic. From *The Broadway Melody* to *Rocky Horror* to *La La Land*, the smart ones have determined how crucial song placement is to a film's success.

> ### MORE TO SEE
>
> *This Is Spinal Tap* (1984): Rock mockumentary par excellence
>
> *Hedwig and the Angry Inch* (2001): Starring another striking, unconventional protagonist

"Sweet Transvestite": Little Nell, Tim Curry, Patricia Quinn, Richard O'Brien

GREASE

STIGWOOD/CARR/PARAMOUNT, 1978 | COLOR (METROCOLOR)/PANAVISION, 110 MINUTES

DIRECTOR: RANDAL KLEISER   PRODUCERS: ALLAN CARR AND ROBERT STIGWOOD   SCREENPLAY: BRONTÉ WOODARD, ADAPTED FROM THE SCRIPT OF THE MUSICAL PLAY BY JIM JACOBS AND WARREN CASEY   SONGS: WARREN CASEY (MUSIC) AND JIM JACOBS (LYRICS), JOHN FARRAR AND BARRY GIBB (ADDITIONAL SONGS)   CHOREOGRAPHER: PATRICIA BIRCH   STARRING: JOHN TRAVOLTA (DANNY), OLIVIA NEWTON-JOHN (SANDY), STOCKARD CHANNING (RIZZO), JEFF CONAWAY (KENICKIE), EVE ARDEN (PRINCIPAL MCGEE), FRANKIE AVALON (TEEN ANGEL), BARRY PEARL (DOODY), DIDI CONN (FRENCHY), DINAH MANOFF (MARTY), SID CAESAR (COACH CALHOUN)

A high-school greaser and a good girl find romance despite their differences.

At a time when musicals on film were next to extinct, this boisterous piece of pop nostalgia went through the roof. Like *The Sound of Music*, this is a success beyond normal movie parameters. Timing is everything, and few musicals ever landed at so perfect a moment.

Millions of people in the 1970s wanted to look back, and the rock 'n' roll era of the late 1950s and early '60s offered easy comfort. Accordingly, the popular hits of the '70s included *American Graffiti* on film, *Happy Days* on television and, on Broadway, a sleeper called *Grease*.

When it came time to turn *Grease* into a movie, there was added to the mix the charisma of a newly minted megastar. With performing

roots on Broadway and television, John Travolta had just demonstrated sensational dance skills in one of the decade's defining hits, *Saturday Night Fever*. For that film's producers, *Grease* would be something of a follow-up, and as close to a sure thing as possible for any musical at that time. The role of Sandy was reconfigured to suit Australian pop star Olivia Newton-John, and the scrappier '50s beat of the original was deftly interlocked with suggestions of '70s disco.

The key factor, it was determined, would be energy—in the music, the cast, and the dancing. Patricia Birch, who had choreographed the show on Broadway, repeated her duties for the film's expanded canvas, which moved the setting to California from the original's Chicago. With a few veterans (Eve Arden, Sid Caesar, Joan Blondell) added to the young(ish) cast, a modestly budgeted and brightly colored production, and a summertime release, *Grease* took off like gangbusters. Huge crowds of mainly young viewers came to see it again and again, easily making it the top-grossing film of the year.

By some measure, *Grease* is the *Star Wars* of the movie musical—a deeply internalized talisman to be enjoyed over and over by those who saw and loved and perhaps needed it when it was new and they were young, then later to be passed along to children and eventually grandchildren. As with *The Sound of Music* and *Rocky Horror*, its popularity has dictated that subsequent revivals of the stage version be adjusted to better conform to the movie that so many more people know. The reasons for the enthusiasm are plain. There is the catchiness of the music and, once

"Greased Lightning": John Travolta

again, that energy, permeating everything and making sure that the script doesn't go too long without another song, or at least a drag race. There is also the particular nature of the nostalgia: a mashup of the late '50s and early '60s as they seldom were, seen through a '70s sensibility.

Nothing is taken too seriously and nothing has to go beneath the surface, which is a motto *Grease* shares with scads of earlier musicals. It helps, too, that the songs, in both arrangements and sonics, come off less like a traditional film soundtrack than as pop singles, including Newton-John's hit "Hopelessly Devoted to You." There's also Travolta, with his photogenic pout, effortless body language, and demon dance skills, showing exactly how a star can dominate a musical while staying cool.

To say that *Grease* is a joyous and masterfully done cartoon is not meant as any kind of a put-down. On the contrary, *Grease* achieves everything it sets out to do and occupies one corner of the musical's history with a winning smirk and an endless amount of vitality. There's nothing remotely hopeless about that.

Top to Bottom | "Beauty School Drop-Out": Frankie Avalon, Stockard Channing, Didi Conn | "Look at Me, I'm Sandra Dee": Stockard Channing | "Born to Hand Jive": Olivia Newton-John and John Travolta | Sid Caesar and Eve Arden

WHAT'S MORE

A number of pop-fueled imitators came out in the wake of *Grease*, and none was successful. *Sgt. Pepper's Lonely Hearts Club Band*, shot immediately after *Grease*, was a costly flop, and *Can't Stop the Music* (1980), *Xanadu* (1980), and the inevitable *Grease 2* (1982) were all unfortunate and much-derided misfires. In this particular realm of movie musicals, the smash success of *Grease* is, ultimately, the exception to prove the rule.

• • •

Grease shares with other musical hits a large roster of the might-have-beens considered and not cast. Before Travolta was in place, the producers thought about Henry Winkler, Fonzie on *Happy Days*. Early candidates for Sandy included Susan Dey, Marie Osmond, and Deborah Raffin, while Lucie Arnaz was a strong possibility for Rizzo until Arnaz's mother, Lucille Ball, nixed the idea of a screen test. When Stockard Channing was cast as Rizzo, she became, at thirty-three, the oldest of the lead actors playing teenagers.

MUSICALLY SPEAKING

Among several showstoppers, the dance-off at the gym to "Born to Hand Jive" is especially notable for the snappy dancing by Travolta, Annette Charles, and much of the cast. It was shot during a California summer in a real gym that had next to no ventilation and, worse, was next door to a pork-processing plant. Between the stifling heat and the bacon smell, it's hardly surprising that numerous dancers fainted, and a wonder that it all turned out so well.

MORE TO SEE

Little Shop of Horrors (1986): Another cartoonish show, very well done

Hairspray (2007): More nostalgia, Travolta, and high spirits

"Summer Nights": Jeff Conaway, John Travolta, Michael Tucci, Kelly Ward

BEAUTY AND THE BEAST

WALT DISNEY, 1991 | COLOR (TECHNICOLOR), 84 MINUTES

DIRECTORS: GARY TROUSDALE AND KIRK WISE   PRODUCER: DON HAHN   SCREENPLAY: LINDA WOOLVERTON, BASED ON THE STORY BY JEANNE-MARIE LEPRINCE DE BEAUMONT   SONGS: ALAN MENKEN (MUSIC) AND HOWARD ASHMAN (LYRICS)   CAST VOICES: PAIGE O'HARA (BELLE), ROBBY BENSON (BEAST), ANGELA LANSBURY (MRS. POTTS), JERRY ORBACH (LUMIÈRE), DAVID OGDEN STIERS (COGSWORTH), RICHARD WHITE (GASTON), JO ANNE WORLEY (WARDROBE), REX EVERHART (MAURICE), JESSE CORTI (LEFOU), BRADLEY MICHAEL PIERCE (CHIP)

A bookish girl unselfishly takes her father's place as prisoner in the castle of a fearsome beast.

Disney happily goes back to its *Snow White* roots in what is likely the finest full-fledged original, non-adapted musical seen on the screen since *Mary Poppins*.

The success of *The Little Mermaid*, in 1989, made several things clear to both the Disney organization and, pretty much, the rest of the world. One was that the studio could still make animated fairy tales the public would love. Another was that the dearth of movie musicals in the 1980s and '90s need not extend to animated films. A third was that Howard Ashman and Alan Menken were hugely talented songwriters and a perfect match for the Disney style. *Beauty and the Beast*, then, was something of an inevitable follow-up, and had been under consideration by the studio for decades. It differed from previous animated features in having a full-fledged screenplay, not a series of storyboard sequences, as well as an early use of digital technology. By Disney standards, it was a troubled project, with much of the initial animation work being scrapped and the original director resigning. Most tragically, lyricist Ashman died from AIDS-related causes while production was underway. When finally completed, it scored a degree of acclaim nearly equal to that of its greatest animated predecessors, including the first Academy Award nomination for Best Picture given an animated feature. There were also astronomical grosses, a live-action Broadway version that ran for thirteen years, and eventually a hugely expensive and extremely profitable remake that blended live action with digital animation.

From its very opening, it's clear that *Beauty and the Beast* is, proudly and overtly, as much a musical as *The King and I* or *Fiddler on the Roof.* No wonder it moved so easily to the stage—it follows a through-line from the opening scene—setting introduction ("Belle") through the uproarious character exposition of "Gaston," the plot-advancing "Something There" and "The Mob Song," and the showstopping "Be Our Guest." The title song, originally conceived as an up-tempo piece with a rock vibe, was eventually slowed down to a dreamy ballad, then given a definitive rendition (on the first take) by a member of the Broadway musical elite, Angela Lansbury.

As with *The Little Mermaid*, with its happy ending not in the original tale, there are a number of embellishments and changes, some of them not unlike those in Jean Cocteau's classic live-action version, released in 1946. The artwork has considerable richness and detail, the voice characterizations are first-rate, and the musical presentation is as good as any Disney

"Beauty and the Beast"

has ever done. There is also, in the characterization of Belle, a subtly feminist updating that makes her one of the most winning of Disney protagonists. Most particularly, there are those Ashman-Menken songs, as integral to the success of the enterprise as well-executed animation and the special assurance of the Disney brand. Surely one measure of its triumph is the fact that even some of the more effusive reviews of the 2017 Disney version made a point of noting that with an original this good, a remake had not been absolutely necessary.

With both its quality and success, it's small wonder that *Beauty* has paved the way for so many more tales to follow. Many of those, especially *The Lion King* and *Frozen*, have continued along a musical path, but for depth and overall accomplishment, the tale of Belle and her Beast—in this, their original drawn-and-painted incarnations—remains a crowning achievement.

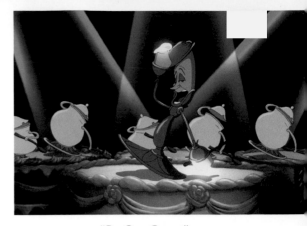

"Be Our Guest"

"The Mob Song"

David Ogden Stiers, Angela Lansbury, and Jerry Orbach in the recording studio

WHAT'S MORE

Ever resourceful and creative, Disney found a way to turn *Beauty*'s production delays into a well-publicized advantage. The film's first public screening, at the New York Film Festival in September 1991, was designated that of a "work in progress," with 30 percent of the film still incomplete. Certain sequences were entirely in pencil outline, while others went back and forth between pencil and full animation. The response was hugely positive, and the unique nature of the project ensured possibly even more attention than it might have gotten as a conventionally finished work.

• • •

The credits of *Beauty and the Beast* include the following, quite appropriate, acknowledgment: "To our friend Howard, who gave a mermaid her voice and a beast his soul, we will be forever grateful. Howard Ashman (1950–1991)."

MUSICALLY SPEAKING

"Be Our Guest" was always intended as a central knock-'em-dead showpiece, serving pretty much the same purpose that "Under the Sea" had in *The Little Mermaid*. Originally, the number was to be performed for Maurice, Belle's father, but after it had been animated the filmmakers realized that Belle would make a more suitable one-person audience. Besides the catchy song itself, it contains a barrage of cinematic references: Maurice Chevalier (expertly channeled by Jerry Orbach), many Warner Bros. and Disney cartoons where objects in a store or kitchen come to life after hours, and especially a great deal of Busby Berkeley. With abstract geometry out of *Dames*, diving beauties from *Footlight Parade* and *Million Dollar Mermaid*, and Berkeley's trademark overhead-camera compositions, this is an overt, breathlessly effective homage. (And would be so again in the 2017 version.) As has been proven again and again, a movie musical can sometimes be most effective when it knows and acknowledges its forebears. Imitation can be flattering, and heartfelt tribute is another, superior, matter entirely.

MORE TO SEE

The Little Mermaid (1989): Ashman-Menken songs and a great villain

South Park: Bigger, Longer & Uncut (1999): A nifty *Beauty* parody in an uproarious animated musical

CHICAGO

MIRAMAX, 2002 | BLACK AND WHITE (NEWSREEL) AND COLOR (DELUXE), 113 MINUTES

DIRECTOR AND CHOREOGRAPHER: **ROB MARSHALL**   PRODUCER: **MARTIN RICHARDS**   SCREENPLAY: **BILL CONDON, BASED ON THE MUSICAL PLAY BY BOB FOSSE AND FRED EBB, FROM THE PLAY BY MAURINE DALLAS WATKINS**   SONGS: **JOHN KANDER (MUSIC) AND FRED EBB (LYRICS)**   STARRING: **RENÉE ZELLWEGER (ROXIE HART), CATHERINE ZETA-JONES (VELMA KELLY), RICHARD GERE (BILLY FLYNN), QUEEN LATIFAH (MATRON MAMA MORTON), JOHN C. REILLY (AMOS HART), CHRISTINE BARANSKI (MARY SUNSHINE), TAYE DIGGS (BANDLEADER), DOMINIC WEST (FRED CASELY), LUCY LIU (KITTY BAXTER), CHITA RIVERA (NICKIE)**

Two murderesses vie for the attention of the press as they await trial in 1920s Chicago.

It was anticipated as few movie musicals had ever been and, wondrously, was worth that endless wait. The icing on the cake came in the first Best Picture Academy Award to go to a musical in thirty-four years.

Chicago's long journey to the screen began with Bob Fosse's original 1975 Broadway production. Its tale of corrupt glamour, even its sensational Kander/Ebb songs, had been overshadowed by the concurrent smash of *A Chorus Line*, and while a movie version might have redressed the matter, few stage musicals were being filmed at the time. Worse still, the ones being filmed often turned out as badly as *The Wiz* or *A Chorus Line*. There was also *Chicago*'s vaudeville-like format, which seemed to discourage a film transfer. For years, there would be talk of a possible production with Goldie Hawn or Liza Minnelli, then nothing. Not even Fosse himself, who once contemplated casting Madonna as Roxie, could get it off the ground. Then, in 1996, an enormously successful Broadway revival proved that, just perhaps, the show had been a little ahead of its time. It was left to director/choreographer Rob Marshall (in his feature film debut) and screenwriter Bill Condon to figure out a way for *Chicago* to work on film. What they laid out was not unlike *Cabaret*: having the songs performed in an overtly theatrical setting, mostly as imagined by the stage-struck Roxie Hart. While the show's final touch of acid was slightly softened, the overall harsh tone remained fairly intact.

Marshall approached *Chicago* in a mega-edited, no-room-for-doubt style that some found overdone; far more felt that the method was a good match for the material. The emphatic music-video style was, in fact, an extremely astute way to draw in younger audiences who had grown up watching quick cuts and fragmented presentation. It was the complete opposite of a Fred Astaire, who attempted to make dance on

"Hot Honey Rag": Catherine Zeta-Jones and Renée Zellweger

film a seamless experience, and quite well suited to a world filled with dancing murderesses, gullible reporters, and crooked attorneys.

There was also, in the cast as in the material, the substance to back up the style. Renée Zellweger fit perfectly into Marshall's concept of Roxie as a desperately game amateur, and Richard Gere's air of self-containment was ideally suited to the truth-optional attorney Billy Flynn. Perhaps most striking was Catherine Zeta-Jones, who up to that time had won superlatives mainly for looking dazzling. As it turned out, she could sing, dance, act, and snarl—all necessities for the role of Velma Kelly.

With Zeta-Jones and the chorus offering an atomic-powered "All That Jazz" at the very outset, *Chicago* could have been in danger of tapering off and fizzling out. Instead, it moved from strength to strength, most notably in Marshall's staging of "We Both Reached for the Gun" and "Cell Block Tango" with, every now and again, references to earlier musical legends. The allusions included Astaire, Kelly, Berkeley, Monroe, Charisse, and, of course, Fosse—a glorious musical past saluted exuberantly by an ambitious and gifted present.

With energy, expertise, and intelligence, *Chicago* proved that musicals weren't dead, and, in fact, need never be when the talent and enterprise are there. As long there are people of this caliber around, audiences will be blessed with more good musicals, and all that jazz.

"When You're Good to Mama": Queen Latifah

Above "And All That Jazz": Catherine Zeta-Jones | **Top Right** "Razzle Dazzle": Richard Gere | **Middle Right** "Cell Block Tango": Catherine Zeta-Jones | **Bottom Right** "Roxie": Renée Zellweger

WHAT'S MORE

Long before it was a musical, *Chicago* had been a hit play (1926), a silent film (1927), and a Ginger Rogers movie titled *Roxie Hart* (1942). Prior to these it was, give or take, pretty much a true story. Reporter-turned playwright Maurine Dallas Watkins based Roxie on a winsome Chicago murderess named Beulah Annan, while the real-life Velma was one Belva Gaertner. Both women won their acquittal in 1924, and Watkins added to the mix by basing Mary Sunshine on herself.

• • •

Because of its lengthy road from stage to film, *Chicago* had an even greater "also-ran" contingent than most musical projects. All were considered, some turned it down, others were given the thumbs-down, and one (Fosse) died. To direct: Bob Fosse, Milos Forman, Herbert Ross, Baz Luhrmann. To star: Goldie Hawn, Toni Collette, Charlize Theron, Nicole Kidman, Liza Minnelli, Madonna, Gwyneth Paltrow, Cameron Diaz, Kristin Chenoweth, John Travolta, Hugh Grant, Kevin Spacey, John Cusack, Steve Martin, Kevin Kline, Kathy Bates, Bette Midler, Whoopi Goldberg, and Rosie O'Donnell. Some good possibilities there, plus a few exclamations of "Really?"

MUSICALLY SPEAKING

Several of the Kander/Ebb songs are quite pointed in striking to the heart of the show's stone-hearted theme, and none more so than "Razzle Dazzle," staged by Marshall as a literal, glitter-and-paint three-ring circus. With its emphasis on criminal justice as show-biz, plus the possibility of high-profile criminals getting away with murder, the number makes an excellent case for the fact that *Chicago* was clairvoyant as well as cynical. It took more than twenty years for a large public to completely grasp the show's premise, and by then the point was clear enough to help make the show a huge hit on film and, on Broadway, the most successful revival in history.

> ### MORE TO SEE
>
> *Pennies from Heaven* (1981): Striking, from director Herbert Ross
>
> *Moulin Rouge!* (2001): Baz Luhrmann's divisive phantasmagoria

Director Rob Marshall and Renée Zellweger on the set

LA LA LAND

SUMMIT ENTERTAINMENT/LIONSGATE, 2016 | COLOR (KODAK VISION3)**/ CINEMASCOPE, 128 MINUTES**

DIRECTOR AND SCREENPLAY: DAMIEN CHAZELLE   PRODUCERS: FRED BERGER, GARY GILBERT, JORDAN HOROWITZ, AND MARK PLATT   SONGS: JUSTIN HURWITZ (MUSIC) AND BENJ PASEK AND JUSTIN PAUL (LYRICS)   CHOREOGRAPHER: MANDY MOORE   STARRING: RYAN GOSLING (SEBASTIAN), EMMA STONE (MIA), JOHN LEGEND (KEITH), ROSEMARIE DEWITT (LAURA), J. K. SIMMONS (BILL), FINN WITTROCK (GREG), TERRY WALTERS (LINDA), TOM EVERETT SCOTT (DAVID), CALLIE HERNANDEZ (TRACY), JESSICA ROTHE (ALEXIS)

A jazz pianist and an aspiring actress find love and career conflict in Los Angeles.

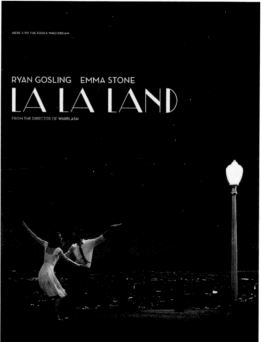

As romantic as the films of Demy, as imaginative as the work of Mamoulian or Berkeley, as formally committed as the best of Minnelli and, simply put, a stunner of a musical love story. Add Damien Chazelle to the list of outstanding musical directors.

Consciously and joyfully, *La La Land* is both determinedly forward-looking and blissfully retro, looking back on the entirety of musical film while it dances toward a bright future. In contrast to the Broadway adaptations preceding it, *La La Land* is, in both its script and its songs, conceived directly for the screen, just like *The Broadway Melody*, *Sunny Side Up*, the Astaire-Rogers films, and *The Umbrellas of Cherbourg*, which is Chazelle's favorite film. The characters of Seb and Mia are surrogates for the movie itself: he's a musician so rooted in jazz's past that he jeopardizes his own present; she's an actor who goes nowhere until she dares to take chances. Similarly, this film knows and uses its origins, yet has enough self-awareness and guts to stretch past the notion of simply a rehash of a glorious past. Chazelle deploys his references with great care: the Day-Glo-in-song vibe of *Umbrellas*, as well as the doomed romance of *A Star Is Born* and Martin Scorsese's fascinating *New York, New York*; "Dancing in the Dark" from *The Band Wagon*, scenes from other Minnelli films, and echoes of *Cover Girl, Singin' in the Rain, Funny Face*, and even a dancing-in-the-sky bit copped from a lesser-known Astaire title, *The Belle of New York*. The homages are evident, yet seem less derivative than affectionate. Like all the best musical films, *La La Land* understands and loves its roots even as it works, determinedly, to find its own way. As with many other major musicals, it is a way that has been much discussed, and for millions remains wholly captivating.

One of the film's most distinctive characteristics is also one of its most endearing assets.

The plain and evident truth is that, in the musical sequences, Gosling and Stone sing and dance like "real people," not Kelly or Crosby or Garland or Charisse. Surely this is an ingenious way of reinforcing the time-honored precept in musicals that, really, anybody should be able and allowed to get up and do it. These two are believable as a couple, the audience wants them to succeed personally and professionally, and the musical sequences expand on their relationship. Then, when the going gets tough, there is less music—until just before the end, with Chazelle's one-two masterstroke. First is Stone's riveting "Audition (The Fools Who Dream)," a wholehearted performance sung live on camera, which cinches Mia's (and Stone's) reach for stardom. Then comes a virtuoso "alternative ending" deliberately reminiscent of the "American in Paris" ballet, as artificial and bright-hued as the original and an achingly poignant portrayal of

"Epilogue": Ryan Gosling and Emma Stone

what might have been. By expressing genuine feeling through outlandishly stylized means, it epitomizes both *La La Land* and, pointedly, everything musicals can do better than any other kind of movie.

Blissfully and even triumphantly, *La La Land* offers audiences the best of both worlds. A deeply felt meditation on what and where the musical film has been, it also presents hope and any number of happy possibilities for its future. The past, as everyone knows, is prologue, and what a pleasure to observe and report that, as this movie makes clear, there's much more to come.

WHAT'S MORE

It was, on February 26, 2017, an Oscar ceremony wind-up like no other: *La La Land* had already been the recipient of the most nominations (fourteen) ever given to a musical, and was given six Academy Awards. Then it was announced as Best Picture, in what was soon called the biggest single snafu in Academy history. The actual winner, it turned out, was the acclaimed coming-of-age drama *Moonlight*. Who could have foreseen that Oscar night for *La La Land* would have a double-edged/bittersweet finish fully equal to the one in the film itself?

• • •

La La Land opens with the logo for Cinema-Scope, the widescreen process first used in 1953 and discontinued in 1967. It was shot in 35mm in the same ratio, 2.55 to 1, as were such early

"Planetarium": Ryan Gosling and Emma Stone

Ryan Gosling

CinemaScope productions as *The Robe*, *How to Marry a Millionaire*, and the first musical shot in the process, *Lucky Me*. It's surely just a coincidence that the star of *Lucky Me*, Doris Day, also starred in the last "official" CinemaScope film before this one, *Caprice*. If neither of those titles is among Ms. Day's better efforts, they are part of that striking roundelay of historical resonance that surrounds *La La Land* and, in many ways, helps to make it so special.

MUSICALLY SPEAKING

Few musicals have led off with a more bracing musical sequence than the spectacular freeway-traffic-jam-dance "Another Day of Sun," shot on the same express-lane ramp used in the movie *Speed*. The song is delightful, Mandy Moore's choreography is endlessly inventive, and the sheer amount of energy at play is quite remarkable. All praise, then, to the planning and coordination that put it all up on the screen, since Damien Chazelle and the cast and crew did the whole thing in an extraordinary two days.

MORE TO SEE

Everyone Says "I Love You" (1996): Woody Allen's delightful sort-of predecessor to *La La Land*

Into the Woods (2014): Stephen Sondheim's fable, impressively filmed by Rob Marshall

Epilogue

From *The Broadway Melody* all the way to *La La Land*, musicals have taken audiences on quite the extravagant ride. This journey has encompassed periods of adventurous experimentation, exhilarating popularity, artistic daring, decadence and oversaturation, and indifferent silence. Because of musicals, audiences were thrilled to see and hear a new art form, cheered during periods of financial hardship, inspired and diverted during times of war, and exasperated when there seemed to be little justification for such work to exist. Given their intimate relationship with viewers, it's hardly surprising that these films elicit fierce affection on the one hand and, often enough, condescension and aversion on the other. Through it all, amid all the changes of style, technique, and attitude, they somehow persist, managing to come back in one form or another both in movie theaters and on home screens. The memorable

The Band Wagaon "Girl Hunt": Fred Astaire and Cyd Charisse

and older titles are replayed for fresh and often adoring viewers, and sometimes there will be a new entrant into that pantheon where the authentically great ones reside.

It would be wonderful to assert that musicals are consistent in their desire and ability to entertain and captivate, but it's an unavoidable fact that sometimes they forget themselves, their goals, the reasons for their existence. When this occurs, they become unnecessary and beside the point. Fortunately, those that are derivative and mediocre will evaporate, while the must-see classics will stand the test of time and endure. That latter group, those in this book, are comparatively small in number, and were made by artists who best understand how a musical must connect with its public. Such a connection can never be done with phone-it-in expedience, nor with greed or cynicism. It takes respect and sincerity as well as artistry, as has been proved over and over with *The Broadway Melody*, *Love Me Tonight*, *An American in Paris*, *Cabaret* and the others. In all of them, gifted and adventurous people can find the proper way to make musicals that are good, grand, or even great, and with

luck will find the audience that deserves them.

One of the happiest propensities of musicals is their eternal willingness to look back at and deploy their own history. By noting their prior achievements, they find ways to move into the future, which is partly why *Singin' in the Rain* remains so special, *Chicago* so successful, and *La La Land* so gratifying. There would be nothing, of course, without forebears, and any musical—or person, for that matter—who believes that the past doesn't matter is being both self-deceiving and incompetent. It's not imitation, it's inspiration. Thus, as this book comes to its close, it can be noted that director Damien Chazelle cited a principal source for some of the ideas that went into creating that explosive freeway song-and-dance with which *La La Land* begins. It was, Chazelle said, Rouben Mamoulian's opening scene of *Love Me Tonight*, with its intoxicating collage of sounds and images. In that decision can be seen a truly stirring and heartening dynamic: by learning from its roots and acknowledging its past, one must-see musical can pay tribute to another. And, happily, the show goes on.

Selected Bibliography

BOOKS

Altman, Rick. *The American Film Musical.* Bloomington: Indiana University Press, 1987.

Andrews, Julie. *Home: A Memoir of My Early Years.* New York: Hyperion, 2008.

Barrios, Richard. *Screened Out: Playing Gay in Hollywood from Edison to Stonewall.* New York: Routledge, 2002.

—*A Song in the Dark: The Birth of the Musical Film*, 2nd ed. New York: Oxford University Press, 2010.

— *Dangerous Rhythm: Why Movie Musicals Matter.* New York: Oxford University Press, 2014.

Bergreen, Lawrence. *As Thousands Cheer: The Life of Irving Berlin.* New York: Viking, 1990.

Bogle, Donald. *Heat Wave: The Life and Career of Ethel Waters.* New York: HarperCollins, 2011.

Bradley, Edwin M. *The First Hollywood Musicals: A Critical Filmography of 171 Features, 1927–32.* Jefferson, NC: McFarland, 1996.

Cohan, Steven. *Incongruous Entertainment: Camp, Cultural Value, and the MGM Musical.* Durham, NC: Duke University Press, 2005.

Croce, Arlene. *The Fred Astaire and Ginger Rogers Book.* New York: Galahad Books, 1972.

Delamater, Jerome. *Dance in the Hollywood Musical.* Ann Arbor, MI: UMI Research Press, 1978.

Dunne, Michael. *American Film Musical Themes and Forms.* Jefferson, NC: McFarland, 2004.

Feuer, Jane. *The Hollywood Musical.* Bloomington: Indiana University Press, 1982.

Fordin, Hugh. *The World of Entertainment! Hollywood's Greatest Musicals.* Garden City, NY: Doubleday & Company, 1975.

Fricke, John. *Judy Garland: A Portrait in Art and Anecdote.* New York: Bullfinch, 2003.

Fricke, John, Jay Scarfone, and William Stillman. *The Wizard of Oz: The Official 50th Anniversary Pictorial History.* New York: Warner Books, 1989.

Fumento, Rocco, ed. *42nd Street*. Madison: University of Wisconsin Press, 1980.

Furia, Philip, and Laurie Patterson. *The Songs of Hollywood*. New York: Oxford University Press, 2010.

Gatiss, Mark. *James Whale: A Biography*. London: Cassell, 1995.

Harvey, Stephen. *Vincente Minnelli*. New York: Museum of Modern Art, 1989.

Haver, Ronald. *A Star Is Born: The Making of the 1954 Movie and Its 1983 Restoration*. New York: Alfred A. Knopf, 1988.

Hess, Earl J., and Pratibha Daholkar. *Singin' in the Rain: The Making of an American Masterpiece*. Lawrence: University Press of Kansas, 2009.

Higham, Charles, and Joel Greenberg. *The Celluloid Muse: Hollywood Directors Speak*. Chicago: Regnery, 1971.

Hischak, Thomas. *Through the Screen Door: What Happened to the Broadway Musical When It Went to Hollywood*. New York: Oxford University Press, 2004.

Hogan, David J. *The Wizard of Oz FAQ: All That's Left to Know about Life According to Oz*. Milwaukee: Applause Theatre & Cinema Books, 2014.

Kaufman, Gerald. *Meet Me in St. Louis*. London: British Film Institute, 1994.

Kennedy, Matthew. *Roadshow! The Fall of Film Musicals in the 1960s*. New York: Oxford University Press, 2014.

Knight, Arthur. *Disintegrating the Musical: Black Performance and American Musical Film*. Durham, NC: Duke University Press, 2002.

Knox, Donald. *The Magic Factory: How MGM Made "An American in Paris."* New York: Prager, 1973.

Kobal, John. *Gotta Sing Gotta Dance: A Pictorial History of Film Musicals*. London: Hamlyn, 1971; rev ed., London: Spring Books, 1983.

Kreuger, Miles. *Show Boat: The Story of a Classic American Musical*. rev. ed. New York: Da Capo Press, 1990.

Layton, James, and David Pierce. *King of Jazz: Paul Whiteman's Technicolor Revue*. Severn, MD: Media History Press, 2016.

Maslon, Laurence. *The Sound of Music Companion*. New York: Simon & Schuster, 2007.

McElhaney, Joe, ed. *Vincente Minnelli: The Art of Entertainment*. Contemporary Approaches to Film and Television Series. Detroit: Wayne State University Press, 2008.

McGilligan, Patrick. *George Cukor: A Double Life*. New York: St. Martin's, 1991.

Mordden, Ethan. *The Hollywood Musical*. New York: St. Martin's, 1981.

— *When Broadway Went to Hollywood*. New York: Oxford University Press, 2016.

Mueller, John. *Astaire Dancing: The Musical Films*. New York: Wings Books, 1985.

Mundy, John. *The British Musical Film*. Manchester, UK: Manchester University Press, 2007.

Rubin, Martin. *Showstoppers: Busby Berkeley and the Tradition of Spectacle*. New York: Columbia University Press, 1993.

Rushdie, Salman. *The Wizard of Oz*. London: British Film Institute, 1992.

Sennett, Ted. *Hollywood Musicals*. New York: Abrams. 1981.

Silverman, Stephen. *Dancing on the Ceiling: Stanley Donen and His Movies*. New York: Alfred A. Knopf, 1996.

Spivak, Jeffrey. *Buzz: The Life and Art of Busby Berkeley*. Lexington: University of Kentucky Press, 2010.

Williams, Esther, and Digby Deihl. *The Million Dollar Mermaid*. New York: Simon & Schuster, 1999.

PERIODICALS

Billboard

Films in Review

Harrison's Reports

Los Angeles Times

Motion Picture

The Nation

New York

The New York Times

The New Yorker

Photoplay

Sight and Sound

Time

Vanity Fair

Variety

OTHER SOURCES

All Talking! All Singing! All Dancing! A celebration of the early talkies and their times: www.talkieking.blogspot.com.

Box Office Mojo: www.boxofficemojo.com.

The Internet Movie Database: www.imdb.com.

The Eddie Mannix Ledger (MGM Costs and Grosses). The Howard Strickling Collection, Margaret Herrick Library, Academy of Motion Picture Arts and Sciences.

Media History Digital Library: www.mediadigitalproject.org

Motion Picture Association of America. Production Code Administration Records. Margaret Herrick Library, Academy of Motion Picture Arts and Sciences.

Once Upon a Time: The Umbrellas of Cherbourg. 2008 Folamour-TCM documentary, directed by Marie Genin and Serge July.

Rotten Tomatoes: www.rottentomatoes.com.

Turner Classic Movies: www.tcm.com.

Warner Bros. Archive. University of Southern California.

INDEX

Acknowledgments

Few activities can provide more contradictions than writing a book. On the one hand, it must, without question, be a solitary task. Like great musicals, concentration is rare and precious and never to be taken for granted, and it's difficult to imagine writing taking place outside some kind of author's shell. Don't ever pretend, however, that the solitary nature of the writing extends to the job of putting a book together. There, one must always have the advisors and editors and friends and sources of wisdom, knowledge, expertise, criticism, comfort, inspiration, and enthusiasm. Thus it is that this book, like most or all books, was made possible by a number of people, even apart from those artists who are celebrated in its pages.

It goes without saying that this book would never have happened without Turner Classic Movies. That statement could be extended to include not just this book but many people's love of classic films. TCM has been a joy and a treasure for well over two decades, and it has been my great joy and pleasure to renew an association with TCM that originally began in 2007, when I co-hosted a film series based on my book *Screened Out*. It must also be mentioned that I, along with everyone else, suffered a huge loss with the death of the network's public face and host, Robert Osborne. The fact that Bob passed away just as I was finishing this book has made me reflect on how peculiarly the currents of history can operate. More important, it was a reminder of what a masterful host Bob was, what a peerless friend of film, and happily, in my case, what an extraordinary colleague. Thank you, Bob, for all you have meant, and will continue to mean, to all of us. Among many other terrific people at TCM, I would especially like to thank John Malahy, Heather Margolis, Jennifer Dorian, and Genevieve McGillicuddy. Their work, and that of their associates, makes TCM what it is, and made my own work here both viable and enjoyable.

Turner Classic Movies is, of course, a major ongoing source (and shrine) for film, and beyond it I must extend my thanks to all the archives, companies, organizations, and studios who have rescued, cared for, and preserved classic films. Many film preservationists have gone above and beyond the normal parameters to make sure that obscure, sometimes lost, films are saved and made available. To them, and to everyone who helps to fund their endeavors, a special thank-you. Gratitude also to the libraries and archives that have cared for our past and made it available to researchers. And to the websites and blogs that so often now make it possible to do research and investigation without having to venture out too far or too drastically.

Some people, myself emphatically included, may often find that disappointment or disillusionment seem to hover nearby when some aspect of the creative process is not going well. It is my good fortune, then, that most often I can lift myself out of those doldrums by reflecting on those who have enriched my life both professionally and personally. Their wisdom has enhanced my work consistently, their opinions have helped me immensely, and their care and interest have sustained me and my work. There are far too many to name, but I must mention some of those who have helped me in more ways than I can enumerate. In New York: Edward and Mary Maguire, John and Roseann Forde, the Rev. Amy Gregory and Bill Phillips, Joseph Gallagher, Moshe Bloxenheim, Marc Miller, Karen Hartman, Edward Walters, Jeremey Stuart de Frishberg, Jane Klain, Adele Greene, William Grant and Patrick Lacey, Joe McElhaney, Howard Mandelbaum and Photofest, Lou Valentino, Bob Gutowski, Michael Portantiere, and many others. In Connecticut, Lou and Sue Sabini, Chip Reed, and Chris Fray. In Louisiana: my sister, the Rev. Peggy Foreman, and Jared, Luke, Andrew, Nathan, and Zachary Foreman; the Rev. Ned Pitre, Keith Matherne and Spencer Gauthreaux, Keith Caillouet, Darren Guin, and my family, friends, and former classmates. In Texas: Karen Latham Everson, Dr. Melanie Mitchell, and Joe and Katie Mitchell. In Pennsylvania: Beverly and the late Payson Burt and their family, Mike and Vanessa Olsen, Janet Kovacs, David Litofsky, and Janine Lieberman. In Georgia: Christopher Connelly and James Goodwynne, Lee Tsiantis, and Dennis Millay. In New Jersey: among many other good friends and neighbors, Cindy and Hal Robertson, Rosalind and Lawrence Bulk, Amy, Paul, and Eliza Bent, Joann Carney, Beth Haywood, Patrice Nissan Granaldi and her family, Marsha Bancroft, and Pastor Heidi Bak, and my friends and fellow parishioners at Beverly Methodist and at Meals of Love. In the United Kingdom: the Rev. Francesca Rhys, Diane Allen, and Andrew Henderson. In Sweden, Jonas Nordin. In Australia, Paul Brennan. In Brazil, Aureo Chiesse Brandão. And, of course, my sincere appreciation to all my other friends, advisors, colleagues, and confidantes.

Mark A. Vieira is a writer, artist, and film historian of truly remarkable gifts and achievements, and I cannot state enough that this book would not have happened without him. Speaking of indispensable, my deep gratitude to Running Press and the Hachette Book Group for supporting and believing in me. My special thanks, at Running Press, to Josh McDonnell, Kristin Kiser, Seta Zink, and Katie Hubbard. My editor, Cindy De La Hoz has been a bright beacon throughout this project, a constant source of guidance and wisdom and enthusiasm, pointing out directions and giving comfort and advice and leading me to stay on track. I cannot thank you enough, Cindy. Then, finally, my gratitude and love to Jeffrey Smith, whose presence, support, help, and interest make so many things possible and feasible. This book is one of those things, and the list just keeps going and growing.

Again, thanks to all of you, and to all those people who made these films, and these memories, in the first place.